Statistics 1
for Edexcel

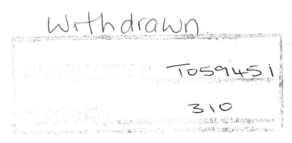

CAMBRIDGE
UNIVERSITY PRESS

The School Mathematics Project

SMP AS/A2 Mathematics writing team David Cassell, Spencer Instone, John Ling, Paul Scruton, Susan Shilton, Heather West

SMP design and administration Melanie Bull, Carol Cole, Pam Keetch, Nicky Lake, Cathy Syred, Ann White

The authors thank Sue Glover for the technical advice she gave when this AS/A2 project began and for her detailed editorial contribution to this book. The authors are also very grateful to those teachers who commented in detail on draft chapters.

PUBLISHED BY THE PRESS SYNDICATE OF THE UNIVERSITY OF CAMBRIDGE
The Pitt Building, Trumpington Street, Cambridge, United Kingdom

CAMBRIDGE UNIVERSITY PRESS
The Edinburgh Building, Cambridge CB2 2RU, UK
40 West 20th Street, New York NY 10011–4211, USA
477 Williamstown Road, Port Melbourne, VIC 3207, Australia
Ruiz de Alarcón 13, 28014 Madrid, Spain
Dock House, The Waterfront, Cape Town 8001, South Africa

http://www.cambridge.org/

© The School Mathematics Project 2004
First published 2004
Reprinted 2009

Printed in the United Kingdom at the University Press, Cambridge

Typeface Minion   *System* QuarkXPress®

A catalogue record for this book is available from the British Library

ISBN 0 521 60535 0 paperback

Typesetting and technical illustrations by The School Mathematics Project

The authors and publisher are grateful to London Qualifications Limited for permission to reproduce questions from past Edexcel examination papers and the statistical tables on pages 120-121. Individual questions are marked Edexcel. London Qualifications Limited accepts no responsibility whatsoever for the accuracy or method of working in the answers given.

Using this book

Apart from chapter 8, which is a review of statistical modelling approaches, each chapter has the following structure.

It begins with a **summary** of what the student is expected to learn.

The chapter then has sections lettered A, B, C, … (see the contents overleaf). In most cases a section consists of development material, worked examples and an exercise.

The **development material** interweaves explanation with questions that involve the student in making sense of ideas and techniques. Development questions are labelled according to their section letter (A1, A2, …, B1, B2, …) and answers to them are provided.

D Some development questions are particularly suitable for discussion – either by the whole class or by smaller groups – because they have the potential to bring out a key issue or clarify a technique. Such **discussion questions** are marked with a bar, as here.

K **Key points** established in the development material are marked with a bar as here, so the student may readily refer to them during later work or revision. Each chapter's key points are also gathered together in a panel after the last lettered section.

The **worked examples** have been chosen to clarify ideas and techniques, and as models for students to follow in setting out their own work. Guidance for the student is in italic.

The **exercise** at the end of each lettered section is designed to consolidate the skills and understanding acquired earlier in the section. Unlike those in the development material, questions in the exercise are denoted by a number only.

Starred questions are more demanding.

After the lettered sections and the key points panel there may be a set of **mixed questions**, combining ideas from several sections in the chapter; these may also involve topics from earlier chapters.

Every chapter ends with a selection of **questions for self-assessment** ('Test yourself').

Included in the mixed questions and 'Test yourself' are **past Edexcel exam questions**, to give the student an idea of the style and standard that may be expected, and to build confidence.

Contents

1 Organising data

In this chapter you will learn how to
• represent data using stem-and-leaf diagrams, histograms and box plots
• find and use the median and quartiles of a set of data
• use interpolation to estimate values

A Organising data by grouping (answers p 122)

People collect data for a purpose – to help answer questions about the real world. They have to decide what data they need to collect and how to process it so that it provides answers to their questions.

For example, the people living in a village want to know whether putting up a sign saying 'Please drive carefully through our village' will make any difference to drivers' speeds. They employ an investigator to measure the speeds of cars as they pass through the village, before and after a sign is put up.

The investigator has to be careful about the choice of the times when she will record the speeds. For example, if she records speeds on a bright day before the sign goes up and on a dark day after, then she will not be able to tell whether any difference in speed is caused by the sign or by the weather. So she tries as far as possible to carry out both sets of measurements under the same conditions.

She decides to record speeds of cars during the same one-hour period on two similar days. Here are the results, in miles per hour (m.p.h.).

Before

32 25 54 61 24 30 48 58 31 40 71 62
42 20 45 36 19 26 68 56 39 45 47 63
25 48 62 55 38 56 42 55 52

After

51 22 18 30 35 64 56 32 43 50 62 73
44 11 23 45 47 39 25 65 53 51 67 32
30 40 28 32 47 29

This is the **raw data** – the data as collected. It is not easy to compare speeds from these lists.

A simple method of organising data is to use a **stem-and-leaf diagram**. This can be drawn for a single set of data or, as in this case, back-to-back.

In the 'after' data, $|6|2$ means 62. In each row the units digits are written in numerical order.

In the 'before' data, $2|5|$ means 52. In each row the units digits are written in numerical order, starting from the right.

Before		After
9	1	1 8
6 5 5 4 0	2	2 3 5 8 9
9 8 6 2 1 0	3	0 0 2 2 2 5 9
8 8 7 5 5 2 2 0	4	0 3 4 5 7 7
8 6 6 5 5 4 2	5	0 1 1 3 6
8 3 2 2 1	6	2 4 5 7
1	7	3

Key

2	5	means 52
	6 2	means 62

A1 Do you think speeds are, on the whole, greater or less after the sign is put up? What feature of the diagram leads you to your answer?

When you make a stem-and-leaf diagram, you do it in two stages.
First you put each 'leaf' (usually the units digit) into the appropriate row.
Then you redo the diagram with the leaves in numerical order.

A2 Here are the marks (out of 100) of a group of students in two maths papers,
paper 1 and paper 2.

Paper 1

42 56 33 40 54 62 26 33 39 45
48 65 50 21 37 42 53 44 60 56
47 24 39 68 35

Paper 2

41 34 37 65 54 42 40 23 52 55
63 67 59 30 25 55 45 71 37 41
64 57 48 65 54

(a) Make a back-to-back stem-and-leaf diagram for the two sets of marks.

(b) Which paper was harder? How does the diagram show this?

Numerical data is of two types, **discrete** and **continuous**. In discrete data the possible
values are separated by gaps, for example 0, 1, 2, 3, ... or shoe sizes 5, $5\frac{1}{2}$, 6, $6\frac{1}{2}$, ...
Continuous data comes from measurement; for example, the speed of a car could be
42.346 57... m.p.h. In practice, measurements can only be recorded to a certain
degree of accuracy and the data will appear to be discrete, as in the car speeds data
on the opposite page. A speed recorded as 37 m.p.h. could be anything between
36.5 and 37.5.

Grouping is a common way of organising data. In the stem-and-leaf diagram
for the car speeds, the data is organised into the groups 10–19, 20–29, ...

Because the speeds were rounded, the 10–19 group contains all speeds in the
interval 9.5–19.5, and so on. The table below shows the frequency for each interval
in the 'before' data set. There is now no gap between each interval and the next.

Speed (m.p.h.)	9.5–19.5	19.5–29.5	29.5–39.5	39.5–49.5	49.5–59.5	59.5–69.5	69.5–79.5
Frequency	1	5	6	8	7	5	1

The data can be shown in a frequency bar chart, using the intervals in the table.

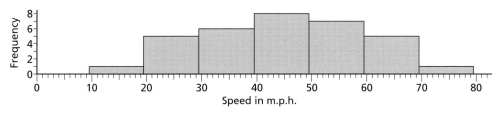

Suppose that it is suggested that the last two groups should be combined into a
single group 59.5–79.5 with a total frequency of 6. The chart would look like this.

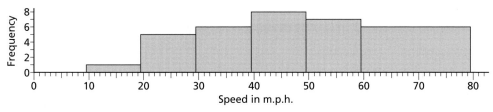

A3 What is wrong with this chart?

The second chart on the previous page is misleading because the eye is drawn to the area rather than the height of the bars.

A chart in which area, not height, shows frequency is called a **histogram**.

The vertical scale on a histogram shows **frequency density** $= \dfrac{\text{frequency}}{\text{width of interval}}$.

Here is the table for the 'before' car speeds data with the last two groups combined, showing the frequency density for each interval.

Speed (m.p.h.)	9.5–19.5	19.5–29.5	29.5–39.5	39.5–49.5	49.5–59.5	59.5–79.5
Frequency	1	5	6	8	7	6
Frequency density	0.1	0.5	0.6	0.8	0.7	0.3

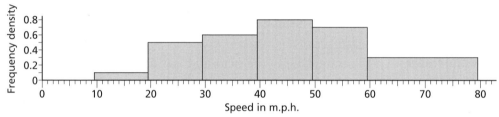

width of interval = 10
frequency density $= \frac{1}{10} = 0.1$

width of interval = 20
frequency density $= \frac{6}{20} = 0.3$

The histogram is shown here.

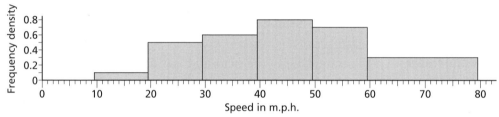

The frequency for each interval is found by multiplying the width of the interval by the frequency density.

For example, the frequency for the interval 59.5–79.5 = width of interval × frequency density
$$= 20 \times 0.3 = 6$$

K

In a histogram, area represents frequency.

The vertical scale shows frequency density $= \dfrac{\text{frequency}}{\text{width of interval}}$

The frequency for an interval = width of interval × frequency density

A histogram shows the distribution of the data. The histogram above shows that the speeds are concentrated towards the middle of the range, with fewer at each end.

Example 1

This histogram shows the distribution of the lengths of phone calls made from a telesales office one evening.

(a) How many calls were made that lasted

    (i) up to 5 seconds   **(ii)** up to 15 seconds

(b) Estimate the number that lasted more than 20 seconds.

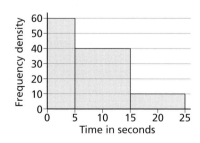

Solution

(a) Area from 0 to 5 $= 5 \times 60 = 300$ calls

(b) Area from 0 to 15 $= 300 + 10 \times 40 = 700$ calls

(c) Assume that the calls in the 15–25 interval are evenly spread.
Area from 20 to 25 $= 5 \times 10 = 50$ calls

Example 2

This is a grouped frequency table for the weights,
to the nearest 10 g, of parcels sent from an office one day.

Draw a histogram to show the data.

Weight (g)	Frequency
50–100	9
110–120	10
130–150	18
160–200	12
210–250	4

Solution

*The weights have been rounded to the nearest 10 g.
So first replace each grouping by a continuous interval.
Then, using the lengths of these intervals, calculate each
frequency density.*

Weight (g)	Frequency	Frequency density
45–105	9	$\frac{9}{60} = 0.15$
105–125	10	$\frac{10}{20} = 0.5$
125–155	18	$\frac{18}{30} = 0.6$
155–205	12	$\frac{12}{50} = 0.24$
205–255	4	$\frac{4}{50} = 0.08$

The histogram is shown below.

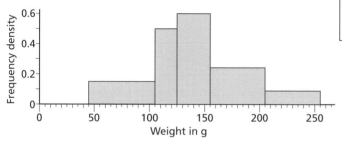

Exercise A (answers p 122)

1 A class of students is given a test. The students' marks are shown below.

```
66  43  46  54  74  37  66  59  40
65  55  57  32  45  59  52  67  83
72  43  84  54  48  78  63
```

(a) Draw a stem-and-leaf diagram for these marks.

(b) What percentage of the students scored fewer than 50 marks in the test?

(c) When a similar test was given to last year's students, the top 20% of
students scored 76 marks or more.
What is the corresponding mark for the top 20% this year?

2 As part of a selection process, 103 employees of a large company were given a task. The times taken to complete the task were recorded to the nearest minute and the following grouped frequency table was made.

Time (minutes)	Frequency
5–9	18
10–14	28
15–24	24
25–39	24
40–49	9

Draw a histogram to show this data.

3 A geography student carries out a survey of house plot sizes in an area of the country. She records the areas of the plots to the nearest 0.1 hectare and produces this grouped frequency table of her results.

Area (hectares)	Frequency
1.0–1.9	15
2.0–2.9	22
3.0–4.9	25
5.0–7.9	16
8.0–9.9	12

Draw a histogram to show this data.

4 This histogram gives information about the weekly earnings of the employees of a company.

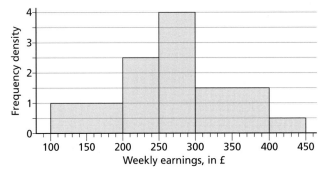

(a) How many employees earn between £250 and £300 a week?

(b) How many employees earn less than £250 a week?

(c) Estimate the number of employees who earn between £175 and £275 a week.

(d) What percentage of the employees earn £400 or more a week?

B Organising data by ordering (answers p 122)

A simple way of organising a set of data is to write it in order, lowest to highest.
Here is the 'before' set of car speeds data from section A, written in order.

19 20 24 25 25 26 30 31 32 36 38 39 40 42 42 45 ㊺ 47 48 48 52 54 55 55 56 56 58 61 62 62 63 68 71

The middle value in this list (ringed) is called the **median** speed.
It can be used as an 'average' of the data.

There is an even number of values in the 'after' set of speeds, so there is no
middle value. However, there is a middle pair of values, and the median is taken
to be halfway between these two.

11 18 22 23 25 28 29 30 30 32 32 32 35 39 ⟨40 43⟩ 44 45 47 47 50 51 51 53 56 62 64 65 67 73

$$\text{Median} = 41.5$$

The fact that the first median is greater than the second suggests that on the whole
the road sign has caused a reduction in speed.

Another feature of interest is the 'spread' of the data. The simplest way to measure
spread is by the **range**, defined as the difference between the highest and lowest values.

The range of the 'before' data is $71 - 19 = 52$. The range of the 'after' data is $73 - 11 = 62$.
This suggests that the 'after' speeds are much more spread out than the 'before' speeds.

However, data sets often contain individual extreme values at the lower or upper ends
that can distort the overall picture. For this reason the **quartiles** are defined.

> The lower, or **first quartile**, Q_1, has $\frac{1}{4}$ of the data values less than or equal to it.
>
> The upper, or **third quartile**, Q_3, has $\frac{3}{4}$ of the data values less than or equal to it.
>
> The median itself is the **second quartile**, Q_2.

When the number of data values is a multiple of 4, for example 12, then Q_1 and Q_3
are found like this.

Find $\frac{1}{4}$ of $12 = 3$. Q_1 is halfway between the 3rd and 4th values.

Find $\frac{3}{4}$ of $12 = 9$. Q_3 is halfway between the 9th and 10th values.

1st 2nd 3rd	4th 5th 6th	7th 8th 9th	10th 11th 12th

When the number of data values is not a multiple of 4, find $\frac{1}{4}$ and $\frac{3}{4}$ of it and
round up to the next positions. For example, with 33 data values

$\frac{1}{4}$ of $33 = 8\frac{1}{4}$, so Q_1 is the 9th value. $\frac{3}{4}$ of $33 = 24\frac{3}{4}$, so Q_3 is the 25th value.

B1 Find the quartiles of each set of car speeds above.

> The difference $Q_3 - Q_1$, is called the **interquartile range**.
> It tells us the spread of the 'middle half' of the data.
> As this excludes extreme values, it is a better measure of spread than the simple range.

For the data sets above, the interquartile ranges are

before: $56 - 32 = 24$ after: $51 - 30 = 21$

On the basis of the interquartile range, the 'before' data set is more spread out.

B2 Find the median, lower quartile and upper quartile for each of these ordered data sets.

(a) 27 33 37 41 43 44 45 47 48 48 49 52 52 54 58 62 69 73 75 79

(b) 35 39 42 47 52 53 54 57 59 60 62 64 66 72 78 83 86

(c) 16 18 20 21 22 25 27 30 33 33 34 37 41 42 44 46 47 48 49 52 55 55 58

(d) 24 25 29 30 31 32 34 36 38 39 39 42 43 44 47 49 52 54

B3 This stem-and-leaf diagram gives the marks of some students in an exam. Find

(a) Q_2

(b) Q_1

(c) Q_3

(d) the interquartile range

```
2 | 2 4 5            (3)
3 | 0 1 3 5 7        (5)
4 | 1 4 4 6 6 8 9    (7)
5 | 2 3 4 6 6 8 8 9  (8)
6 | 1 2 4 7          (4)
7 | 0 3              (2)
```

2|4 means 24

The median and quartiles can be shown in a **box plot**. The box plot for the 'before' car speeds data is shown below. The ends of the box show Q_1 and Q_3, the line inside the box shows the median Q_2, and the ends of the two 'whiskers' show the lowest and highest values in the data.

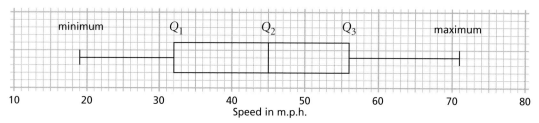

B4 How is the interquartile range shown in the box plot?

B5 Draw a box plot for the 'after' car speeds data.

D **B6** The two box plots below show the distributions of marks in two exams.

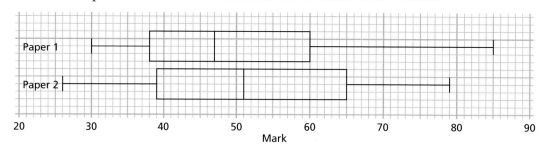

Write a couple of sentences comparing the two sets of marks.

Outliers

An **outlier** in a data set is an exceptionally high or low value. The word 'exceptionally' is vague, so rules have been developed to identify outliers.

One common rule is 'Tukey's rule', named after the American statistician John Tukey (1915–2000). This rule identifies an outlier as any value which is more than ($1.5 \times$ interquartile range) beyond the lower or upper quartile.

For example, if $Q_1 = 45$ and $Q_3 = 67$, the interquartile range is $67 - 45 = 22$. An outlier would be any value less than $45 - 1.5 \times 22$, which is 12, or any value greater than $67 + 1.5 \times 22$, which is 100.

These values 12 and 100, beyond which values become outliers, are sometimes called lower and upper 'fences'.

(There are other versions of the rule in which the multiplier 1.5 is varied.)

When a data set includes one or more outliers, the box plot is modified. The outliers are shown as isolated dots or crosses and the whiskers are drawn up to the lowest and highest data values excluding the outliers.

Example 3

A student measures the pulse rate, in beats per minute, of 50 students at his school and lists them in rank order as follows.

```
34  52  61  62  62  63  64  64  65  65  66  68  68  70  72
73  75  77  77  78  78  79  79  80  80  80  81  81  83  83
84  84  84  85  86  87  89  89  90  90  91  91  93  94  95
99 101 108 122 123
```

The median of this data is 80 and the lower and upper quartiles are 68 and 89.

Identify any outliers using Tukey's rule and use this information to draw a box plot showing the outliers.

Solution

The interquartile range is $89 - 68 = 21$.

Outliers at the lower end are values less than $68 - 1.5 \times 21 = 36.5$.
Outliers at the upper end are values greater than $89 + 1.5 \times 21 = 120.5$.

So 34 at the lower end and 122 and 123 at the upper end are outliers.

Leaving out the outliers, the minimum and maximum values are 52 and 108. This is the box plot for this data.

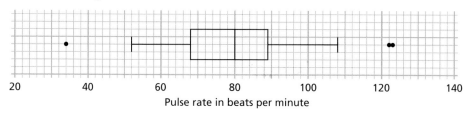

Pulse rate in beats per minute

If, after an outlier has been excluded, there is not enough information to identify the maximum or minimum value of the remaining data, then the whisker is made to end at the 'fence', as in the following example.

Example 4

The prices of flats in a district range from a minimum of £48k to a maximum of £152k. The values of Q_1, Q_2 and Q_3 are £82k, £92k and £106k.

An outlier is defined as any value below $Q_1 - 1.5 \times (Q_3 - Q_1)$ or any value above $Q_3 + 1.5 \times (Q_3 - Q_1)$.

(a) Determine whether the minimum and maximum prices are outliers.

(b) Draw a box plot for the data.

Solution

(a) $Q_1 - 1.5 \times (Q_3 - Q_1) = 82k - 1.5 \times (106k - 82k) = 46k$
So the minimum value, £48k, is not an outlier.

$Q_3 + 1.5 \times (Q_3 - Q_1) = 106k + 1.5 \times (106k - 82k) = 142k$
So the maximum value, £152k, is an outlier.

(b) As the minimum value, £48k, is not an outlier, the lower whisker extends to £48k.

As the maximum value, £152k, is an outlier, the upper whisker extends to the upper fence, £142k.

Q_2 (the median) = £92k. The box plot is shown here.

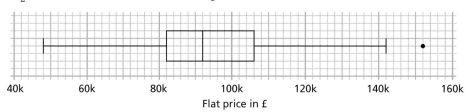

Flat price in £

Exercise B (answers p 122)

1 The weights in kilograms of 14 students are

48.4 47.3 50.4 55.7 52.3 48.2 50.7 44.5 49.2 56.5 52.3 51.5 48.8 55.7

Find the median weight of these students.

2 A citizens' aid charity opened 25 drop-in advice centres in a part of the country. The numbers of callers on the first day of opening are recorded here in order of size.

Find the values of the quartiles Q_1, Q_2 and Q_3 and the interquartile range.

6	10	18	19	23
26	29	30	31	31
33	34	35	36	36
37	38	40	43	44
50	54	56	62	66

3 This stem-and-leaf diagram shows the number of minutes that Albion Railways trains were late arriving at their destination on one day.

(a) Find the values of Q_1, Q_2 and Q_3.

(b) What is the interquartile range?

```
0 | 0 0 0 1 3 4 6 7 7 9
1 | 2 2 4 5 5 7 8 8
2 | 1 3 5 6 6 7 9
3 | 3 4 6 9 9
4 | 2 3
```

1	**2 means 12**

4 A biologist measured the unstretched lengths in cm of 60 earthworms and drew the box plot below to show the results.

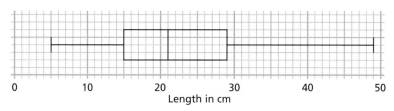
Length in cm

A partially drawn histogram of this data is shown below.

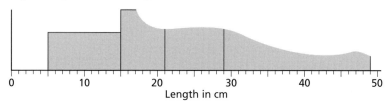
Length in cm

Find the frequency density for each of the four intervals.

5 Some students enter a music exam. Their marks are as shown below.

```
57  33  54  43  47  52  55  40  77  58
69  49  50  55  43  35  51  73  58  60
80  50  37  46  67  85  44  39  47
```

(a) Make a stem-and-leaf diagram to show these marks.

(b) Find the values of Q_1, Q_2 and Q_3.

(c) An outlier is defined as any value x such that $x < Q_1 - 1.5(Q_3 - Q_1)$ or $x > Q_3 + 1.5(Q_3 - Q_1)$.

Determine which of the marks, if any, are outliers.

(d) Draw a box plot for the students' marks.

(e) In another school a similar number of students entered for the same exam. A box plot of their marks is shown below.

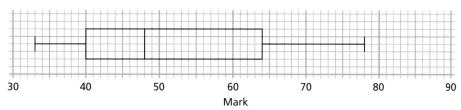
Mark

Use the two box plots to compare the performances of the two groups of students.

C Linear interpolation (answers p 123)

Linear interpolation is a method of estimating unknown values that lie between known values.

Here is the grouped frequency table and histogram for the weights of the parcels sent from an office (as in example 2 on page 9).

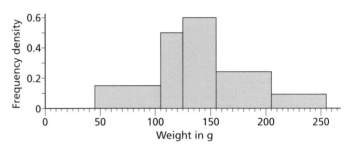

Weight (g)	Frequency
50–100	9
110–120	10
130–150	18
160–200	12
210–250	4

The total number of parcels is 53, so the median is the weight of the 27th parcel. But because the original data values have been lost in the grouping, it is not possible to identify the median.

However, adding the frequencies from the top of the table, we find that the 27th parcel is in the 130–150 group.

This group of 18 parcels is represented by the area of the third bar in the histogram, which is on the interval 125–155. (The interval is 125–155 rather than 130–150 because the weights of the parcels were rounded.)

The bars to the left of this bar account for 19 parcels.

So the third bar represents parcels numbers 20 up to 37.
Parcel number 27 is the 8th in this group of 18.

If we assume that the parcels are evenly spread through the group, then the 27th parcel is $\frac{8}{18}$ of the way across the bar. (See diagram.)

So we can estimate that the median weight is $\frac{8}{18}$ of the way between

125 g and 155 g, which is $125 + \frac{8}{18} \times 30 = 138$ g (to the nearest gram).

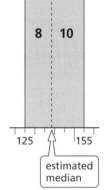

It is not necessary to draw the histogram to use this method, provided that you remember to adjust the intervals to be continuous if the data has been rounded.

C1 This is a frequency table of the lengths, to the nearest minute, of phone calls made from an office one day.

Estimate the median length of a call.

Length (min)	Frequency
0–2	8
3–5	11
6–9	16
10–15	14
16–20	9
> 20	3

Example 5

This is a frequency table for the heights of 240 female students.

Height (cm)	140–145	145–150	150–155	155–160	160–165	165–170	170–175	175–180	180–185
Frequency	3	10	21	54	72	48	25	5	2

Estimate the upper quartile of the heights.

Solution

$\frac{3}{4}$ of $240 = 180$

The intervals in this case are already continuous.

Adding the frequencies up from the start of the table shows that the 180th student is in the interval 165–170.
The groups below this account for 160 students, leaving 20 to get to the 180th.

So the 180th student is 20th out of 48 in the interval 165–170.

Assuming equal spacing, the upper quartile is $165 + \frac{20}{48} \times 5 = 167.1 \, \text{cm}$ (to 1 d.p.).

Exercise C (answers p 123)

1 A researcher in a supermarket measured the time customers spent at a checkout. Each customer was timed from when they joined the queue until when they left the checkout.

A frequency table of the times is given here.

Use linear interpolation to estimate the median time spent at the checkout.

Time (t mins)	Frequency
$0 < t \leq 2$	4
$2 < t \leq 4$	7
$4 < t \leq 6$	12
$6 < t \leq 8$	17
$8 < t \leq 10$	10
$t > 10$	5

2 A gardener grew onions in a plot treated with a fertiliser and in another untreated plot.

The fully grown onions were weighed. The table shows the results.

Use linear interpolation to estimate the median weight of each collection of onions and use the results to compare the two collections.

Weight (g)	With fertiliser frequency	Without fertiliser frequency
50–75	6	3
75–100	9	15
100–125	12	18
125–150	21	10
150–175	16	9
175–200	8	4

3 Estimate the values of Q_1, Q_2 and Q_3 for the following data, based on weighing all the animals in a colony to the nearest kilogram.

Weight (kg)	20–24	25–29	30–34	35–39	40–44	45–49	50–54
Frequency	3	10	16	20	10	6	2

D Large data sets: percentiles (answers p 123)

The grouped frequency table below is based on the measurement of 350 sunflower plants six weeks after planting.

The table next to it is a **cumulative frequency** table. Cumulative frequencies are found by adding up the frequencies as you go down the frequency table.

Height (cm)	Frequency
2.5–6.5	10
6.5–10.5	21
10.5–14.5	114
14.5–18.5	105
18.5–22.5	54
22.5–26.5	46

Height (cm)	Cumulative frequency
up to 6.5	10
up to 10.5	31
up to 14.5	145
up to 18.5	250
up to 22.5	304
up to 26.5	350

A **cumulative frequency graph** is drawn by plotting each cumulative frequency against the upper end of its interval (10 against 6.5, 31 against 10.5, and so on).

The shape of the graph between the plotted points is unknown. Using straight lines to join the points is equivalent to assuming that the data values are evenly spread in each interval. (This is the assumption made by the method of linear interpolation – hence its name.)

The median height of a plant is halfway up the data set, or 175 out of 350. (Strictly speaking it is halfway between the 175th and 176th. However, with a data set of this size, the difference is minimal and can be ignored.)

The line on the graph below shows that the median is estimated to be about 15.6 cm.

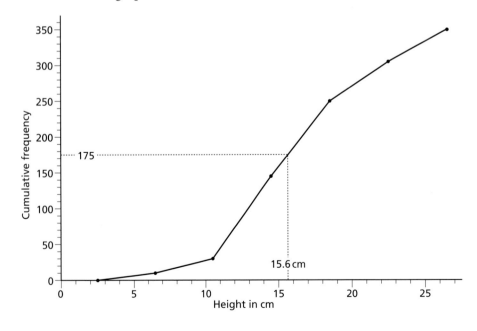

Percentiles

Just as quartiles split the data set into quarters, so **percentiles** split it into hundredths.
The 90th percentile, for example, is the value that has 90% of the data set less than
or equal to it.

90% of 350 = 315, so the 90th percentile can be estimated from the cumulative
frequency graph as shown below.

The other lines show the 25th, 50th and 75th percentiles, which are the first,
second and third quartiles Q_1, Q_2 and Q_3.

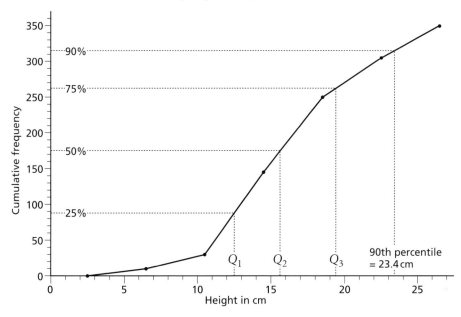

D1 Use the graph to estimate the interquartile range of the heights of the plants.

Unless a data set is large, there is no point in trying to calculate or estimate
percentiles (except for the quartiles).

Exercise D (answers p 123)

1 This cumulative frequency table shows the times
that 150 men spent in hospital after heart attacks.

By drawing a cumulative frequency graph, or by
using linear interpolation without a graph, estimate

(a) the median time spent

(b) the 90th percentile of the times spent

Time (days)	Cumulative frequency
up to 5	40
up to 10	98
up to 15	138
up to 20	144
up to 25	148
up to 30	150

2 A tester measures the lifetimes of 200 batteries of each of two different brands, A and B. The times, in hours, are shown in the frequency table.

Lifetime (hours)	Brand A frequency	Brand B frequency
11.0–11.5	2	8
11.5–12.0	5	14
12.0–12.5	20	43
12.5–13.0	69	50
13.0–13.5	58	48
13.5–14.0	27	30
14.0–14.5	15	5
14.5–15.0	4	2

(a) On the same axes, draw a cumulative frequency graph for each brand.

(b) Use the graphs to estimate the median lifetime for each brand.

The tester expects there to be a few exceptional batteries at both ends of the range. She decides to use the difference between the 90th and 10th percentiles as a measure of the spread.

(c) Use this measure to compare the spread of the lifetimes of the two brands.

Key points

- In a histogram, area represents frequency.
  The vertical scale shows frequency density $= \dfrac{\text{frequency}}{\text{width of interval}}$

  The frequency for an interval = width of interval × frequency density (p 8)

- The median is the middle value (when there is an odd number of data values) or halfway between the middle pair (when there is an even number of data values). (p 11)

- The first quartile, Q_1, has $\frac{1}{4}$ of the data values less than or equal to it.

  The third quartile, Q_3, has $\frac{3}{4}$ of the data values less than or equal to it.

  The median is the second quartile, Q_2.
  The interquartile range is $Q_3 - Q_1$. (p 11)

- If n, the number of data values, is a multiple of 4, then

  Q_1 is halfway between the $\frac{n}{4}$ th and $\left(\frac{n}{4} + 1\right)$th value, and

  Q_3 is halfway between the $\frac{3n}{4}$ th and $\left(\frac{3n}{4} + 1\right)$th values.

  If n is not a multiple of 4, find $\frac{1}{4}n$ and round up to get the position of Q_1; find $\frac{3}{4}n$ and round up to get the position of Q_3. (p 11)

- An outlier is an exceptionally low or high data value. One rule for identifying outliers is: x is an outlier if $x < Q_1 - 1.5(Q_3 - Q_1)$ or $x > Q_3 + 1.5(Q_3 - Q_1)$. (p 13)

- Linear interpolation can be used to estimate a value lying between two known values. (p 16)

- The 90th percentile is the value that has 90% of data values less than or equal to it, and similarly for other percentiles. (p 19)

Test yourself (answers p 123)

1 The numbers of customers for a weekday coach service over the past 9 weeks are shown in this stem-and-leaf diagram.

1	4 6 8 8	(4)
2	3 4 5 5 6 7 8 9	(8)
3	0 1 1 2 2 4 5 5 6 7 8 9 9	(13)
4	2 3 3 4 5 5 6 6 7 8 9	(11)
5	0 0 1 1 1 2 2 2 2	(9)

1 | 4 means 14

(a) Find the values of Q_1, Q_2 and Q_3.

During the previous 9 weeks the values of the quartiles were $Q_1 = 32$, $Q_2 = 40$ and $Q_3 = 46$.

(b) Use the quartiles to compare the two sets of data.

2 The areas, in hectares, of farm fields in a district range from a minimum of 45 to a maximum of 127. The values of Q_1, Q_2 and Q_3 are 76, 90 and 103.

An outlier is defined as any value x such that $x < Q_1 - 1.0 \times (Q_3 - Q_1)$ or $x > Q_3 + 1.0 \times (Q_3 - Q_1)$.

(a) Determine whether the minimum and maximum areas are outliers.

(b) Draw a box plot for the data.

3 The table below shows the distribution of the weights, to the nearest 0.1 kg, of the babies born in a hospital during a 14-day period.

Weight (kg)	2.0–2.9	3.0–3.1	3.2–3.3	3.4–3.5	3.6–3.9	4.0–4.4
Frequency	3	7	10	8	4	2

(a) Draw a histogram to represent the data.

(b) Use linear interpolation to estimate the median weight.

4 Three swimmers Alan, Diane and Gopal record the number of lengths of the swimming pool they swim during each practice session over several weeks. The stem-and-leaf diagram below shows the results for Alan.

Lengths

2	0 1 2 2	(4)
2	5 5 6 7 7 8 9	(7)
3	0 1 2 2 4	(5)
3	5 6 6 7 9	(5)
4	0 1 3 3 3 3 3 4 4 4	(10)
4	5 5 6 6 6 7 7 8 8 9 9 9	(12)
5	0 0 0	(3)

2 | 0 means 20

(a) Find the three quartiles for Alan's results.

This table summarises the results for Diane and Gopal.

(b) Using the same scales and on the same sheet of paper, draw box plots to represent the data for Alan, Diane and Gopal.

(c) Compare and contrast the three box plots.

	Diane	Gopal
Smallest value	35	25
Lower quartile	37	34
Median	42	42
Upper quartile	53	50
Largest value	65	57

Edexcel

2 Summarising data

In this chapter you will learn
- how to find the mean, variance and standard deviation of a set of data
- what is meant by the skewness of a distribution
- how to choose appropriate measures to summarise and compare data sets

A Measures of average (answers p 124)

One of the main purposes of summarising a set of data is to obtain a few measures that can be used to compare one set of data with another.

Measures of average are designed to yield a 'central' value of a set of data.

The **mode** is the simplest of these: it is the value (if there is just one) that occurs most frequently. However, unless the mode occurs sufficiently often it is not a good measure of a central or 'typical' value. For example, in the data set below the mode is 8 but it can hardly be called an 'average' value.

> 7 7 8 8 8 10 15 20 23 24 24 25 26 27 29 32 35 35 40

The mode may be a useful measure when there is a definite concentration of equal values near the middle of a distribution, as here:

> 4 5 7 11 15 17 17 18 18 18 18 19 19 20 25 29 30

However, in general the mode is much less useful than other measures of average.

The **median** is a measure of average. It is easy to calculate, or to estimate if the data has been grouped (see pages 11, 16–17).

The **mean** is also a measure of average. It is defined as the total of all the data values divided by the number of them.

If there are n data values, denoted by $x_1, x_2, x_3, \ldots, x_n$, the mean is denoted by μ ('mu')
and is defined by $\mu = \dfrac{x_1 + x_2 + x_3 + \ldots + x_n}{n}$.

The operation of adding together items of the same kind is met so frequently that it is given a special symbol, Σ (sigma, the Greek capital S, for 'sum').

The definition above is written as $\mu = \dfrac{\Sigma x_i}{n}$ or even more simply as $\mu = \dfrac{\Sigma x}{n}$.

K The mean of a set of n data values $x_1, x_2, x_3, \ldots, x_n$ is $\mu = \dfrac{\Sigma x_i}{n}$.

A1 (a) Find the median and the mean of this data set.

> 4 5 7 10 12 15 17 20 24 26

 (b) What is the effect on the median and on the mean of
   (i) replacing the value 26 by 36
   (ii) adding 5 to each of the last four data values
   (iii) halving the first four data values

The median is not affected by changing the extreme values in a data set. This could be an advantage of using the median as a measure of average, for example if the extreme values are thought to be unreliable or exceptional. In fact many individual values could be changed without affecting the value of the median.

In many circumstances it is better to have a measure that takes all the actual data values into account. The mean does this and is also easier to deal with mathematically as it is defined by a formula. So the mean is the most important measure of average in statistics.

A2 (a) This dot plot shows a small data set. Calculate the mean of the data.

(b) What happens to the mean if

(i) 20 is added to every value

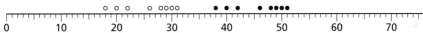

(ii) every value is doubled

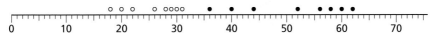

(iii) every value is first doubled and then increased by 20

(iv) every value is first multiplied by 3 and then decreased by 10

K Suppose a data set consists of the n values $x_1, x_2, x_3, \ldots, x_n$ and the mean is μ.
If every value is multiplied by a, the mean is multiplied by a and becomes $a\mu$.
If every value is increased by b, the mean is increased by b and becomes $\mu + b$.
If every value is multiplied by a and then increased by b, the same happens to the mean, which becomes $a\mu + b$.

These facts about the mean can be used to make calculations easier.

A3 A data set consists of the values

    350 370 380 400 430 440

(a) Subtract 300 from every value. Then divide the results by 10. Now find the mean of the numbers you have.

(b) Hence find the mean of the original data set.

A4 Use a similar method to find the mean of this data set.

    21.4 21.5 21.7 21.9 22.1

The methods used in the last two questions are called **coding** the data.

The coding formula in A3 can be written   new value $= \dfrac{\text{original value} - 300}{10}$.

A5 Write down the coding formula you used in A4.

The mean that you get after coding the data has to be converted to the mean of the original data by decoding.

For example, if the coding formula in words is 'subtract 300, then divide by 10', the decoding formula is the inverse: 'multiply by 10, then add 300'.

A6 Here is a data set.

35.4 32.9 40.6 33.8 36.0 34.9

(a) Using the coding $y = 10 \times (\text{original value} - 30)$, write down the six values of y.

(b) Find the mean of the values of y.

(c) Hence find the mean of the original data.

Example 1

These are the prices, in £000, of eight houses in a neighbourhood.

460 575 435 665 550 425 585 445

(a) Code these numbers using the formula $y = \dfrac{\text{price in £000} - 400}{5}$.

(b) Find the mean of the coded data.

(c) Find the mean of the original data.

Solution

(a) The first coded value is $\dfrac{460 - 400}{5} = 12$. The others are 35 7 53 30 5 37 9

(b) Mean of coded data $= \frac{1}{8}(12 + 35 + 7 + 53 + 30 + 5 + 37 + 9) = 23.5$

(c) The coding formula is 'subtract 400, divide by 5'. The inverse is 'multiply by 5, add 400'.
Original mean $= 23.5 \times 5 + 400 = 517.5$ (giving a price of £517 500)

Exercise A (answers p 124)

1 (a) Find the mean of this data set.

1 3 5 7 7 8 8 9

(b) Hence write down the mean of each of these data sets.

(i) 41 43 45 47 47 48 48 49

(ii) 210 230 250 270 270 280 280 290

(iii) –4 –2 0 2 2 3 3 4

(iv) 30 90 150 210 210 240 240 270

(v) 37 97 157 217 217 247 247 277

2 The amount of money, in pounds, taken by a theatre each day in a week was as follows.

240 235 210 270 265 355 380

Use the coding $y = \dfrac{\text{amount in £} - 200}{5}$ to find the mean amount.

3 A biologist measured the widths of the shells of a collection of crabs. He coded the data using the formula $y = 10 \times (\text{width in cm} - 5)$ and found the coded mean to be 47. Find the mean width of the shells.

4 The yearly mileages of the cars in a company's fleet were coded using the formula $y = \dfrac{\text{yearly mileage} - 15\,000}{100}$.

The coded mean is 13.72. Find the mean yearly mileage of the cars.

5 The table shows the lengths and widths of five rectangular swimming pools.

Length (m)	20	25	32	40	45
Width (m)	7	10	14	18	20

Show that multiplying the mean length by the mean width does **not** give the mean area of the pools.

B Measures of spread (answers p 124)

The mean and median are each used as a central or 'average' value for a set of data.
However, on their own they give an incomplete picture of the data.
For example, the two sets of data shown in these histograms have the same mean but are otherwise very different.

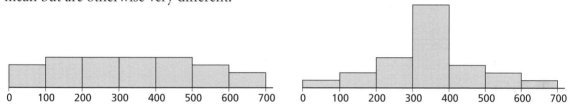

To get a better idea of the distribution of a data set we need a measure of **spread**.

The range is of no use in the example above as it is the same for both data sets.

The interquartile range, which tells us the range of the 'middle half' of the data, is a better measure. The box plots below show the interquartile range for each of the two data sets.

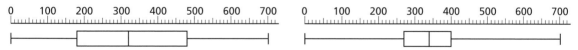

Some data values in a set could be changed without affecting the interquartile range. For example, the extreme values could be increased or decreased without making any difference to the interquartile range. The interquartile range is said to be 'insensitive' to some ways of changing the data.

The same is true of the median as a measure of average. It is insensitive to changes in the data values. The mean, however, is calculated using every individual data value, so is sensitive to changes in data values.

For many purposes a measure of spread is needed that takes account of every individual data value. This is what we shall investigate next.

Some students compared the lengths of laurel leaves on a hedge bordering their school to see if there was a difference between those inside and those outside the school. They took some leaves from the hedge inside the school and some from the outside. These are the lengths of their leaves, measured in centimetres.

Outside	7.9	6.1	7.2	6.0	7.8	7.5	6.3	8.1	7.3	7.4	6.5
Inside	8.5	6.4	7.3	5.7	7.1	6.6	7.4				

This is a dot plot of these results.

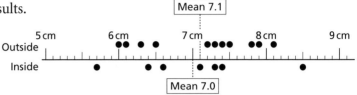

B1 From the dot plot, which leaves appear to have a wider spread, those inside the school or those outside?

Instead of using the interquartile range we can consider the **deviation** of each length from the mean of its group.

For the outside leaves, the deviation of the smallest leaf from the mean is $6.0 - 7.1 = -1.1$ cm. Notice that this deviation is negative because the length is less than the mean.

B2 Find the deviation from the mean of each of the other outside leaves. Suppose it is suggested that the sum of all the deviations could be used as a measure of the spread of the outside leaves. What is wrong with this suggestion?

B3 Find the sum of the deviations from their mean of the lengths for the inside leaves. Does the same thing happen? Can you explain why?

There are two possible ways of using the deviations to measure spread.
- Ignore the sign of the deviations and then add.
- Square the deviations (to get all positive values) and then add.

The first of these is more difficult to handle mathematically, so the second is generally used.

The deviations of the outside leaves are 0.8, −1.0, 0.1, and so on.
Squaring them gives 0.64, 1, 0.01, and so on.

B4 Calculate the sum of the squared deviations for each group of leaves. Is this a useful measure of spread to compare the two sets of data?

To allow for the fact that the two groups have different numbers of items, the sum of the squared differences is divided by the number of items. This measure is called the **variance**.

B5 Calculate the variance of each group of leaf lengths. Which group does the variance suggest has the greater spread?

Because the deviations were squared, the units of the variance are cm^2.
It would be more useful to have a measure of spread in the same units as the data.
By taking the square root of the variance we arrive at a measure called
the **standard deviation**.

B6 Calculate the standard deviation of each group of leaf lengths.

B7 Calculate the mean and standard deviation of these ages of seven children at a
holiday playgroup.

      1 2 2 2 3 5 6

B8 The numbers of eggs laid by some hens each day in a ten-day period were

      4 3 0 1 6 1 3 3 2 4

Find the mean and standard deviation of the number of eggs laid.

The standard deviation is denoted by σ (the small Greek letter sigma),
so the variance is denoted by σ^2.

Using Σ-notation

We have seen that the definition of the mean can be written as $\mu = \dfrac{\Sigma x_i}{n}$.

This notation can also be used for the variance and standard deviation.

The deviations of the data values from the mean are $(x_1 - \mu)$, $(x_2 - \mu)$, $(x_3 - \mu)$, ...

The sum of all the squared deviations can be written as $\Sigma(x_i - \mu)^2$.

The definitions of variance (σ^2) and standard deviation (σ) are

$$\text{variance } \sigma^2 = \frac{\Sigma(x_i - \mu)^2}{n} \qquad \text{standard deviation } \sigma = \sqrt{\frac{\Sigma(x_i - \mu)^2}{n}}$$

These formulae are not the most convenient for calculating σ^2 and σ.
To use them we have to calculate μ first and then subtract it from each value of x.

By using some algebra, an equivalent but more convenient formula can be found.

We have to calculate this sum:

Multiplying out each term gives this:

$$(x_1 - \mu)^2 \qquad x_1^2 - 2\mu x_1 + \mu^2$$
$$+ (x_2 - \mu)^2 \qquad x_2^2 - 2\mu x_2 + \mu^2$$
$$+ (x_3 - \mu)^2 \qquad x_3^2 - 2\mu x_3 + \mu^2$$
$$+ \quad \ldots \qquad\qquad \ldots$$

Adding the terms gives $\Sigma(x_i - \mu)^2 \quad = \quad \Sigma x_i^2 - 2\mu\Sigma x_i + n\mu^2$

However, since $\mu = \dfrac{\Sigma x_i}{n}$, we can replace Σx_i in the second expression by $n\mu$.

This makes the second expression $\Sigma x_i^2 - 2n\mu^2 + n\mu^2 = \Sigma x_i^2 - n\mu^2$.

So σ^2, which by definition is $\dfrac{\Sigma(x_i - \mu)^2}{n}$, is equal to $\dfrac{\Sigma x_i^2 - n\mu^2}{n}$ or $\dfrac{\Sigma x_i^2}{n} - \mu^2$.

The last expression is the easiest one to use.

K To calculate σ^2 and σ use the formulae

$$\sigma^2 = \frac{\sum x_i^2}{n} - \mu^2 \qquad \sigma = \sqrt{\frac{\sum x_i^2}{n} - \mu^2}$$

The first formula can be stated in words as 'variance = mean of squares − square of mean'.

Example 2

These are the ages of the members of a cricket team.

23 37 24 44 30 19 48 36 23 40 29

Calculate the mean and standard deviation of the ages.

Solution

$\mu = \frac{\sum x}{n} = 32.09... = 32.1$ (to 1 d.p.)

$\sigma^2 = \frac{\sum x^2}{n} - \mu^2 = \frac{23^2 + 37^2 + ... + 29^2}{11} - (32.09...)^2 = 82.99...$

So $\sigma = \sqrt{82.99...} = 9.11$ (to 3 s.f.)

Using statistical functions on a calculator or spreadsheet

Most scientific calculators have keys for obtaining the mean and standard deviation of a set of numbers. The mean is usually denoted by $\bar{x}$ or μ and the standard deviation by σ_n. (There is also a key labelled σ_{n-1} which has a different purpose.)

A spreadsheet can also be used. In Excel the functions are

mean: AVERAGE(range of cells)   standard deviation: STDEVP(range of cells)

A spreadsheet can be a useful tool for getting a feel of what the standard deviation tells you about a set of data. You could experiment like this.

Enter a set of numbers that are equally spaced, such as 20, 25, 30, 35, 40, 45, 50. Find the standard deviation. Then make the middle numbers closer to one another, for example, 20, 25, 34, 35, 36, 45, 50 and see what effect this has on the standard deviation. Increase the spacing between numbers and see the effect of this, and any other changes that occur to you. Try to predict what the effect will be before you re-calculate the standard deviation.

Exercise B (answers p 124)

Where possible, use the statistical functions on your calculator, showing the steps you take.

1 The numbers of peas in fourteen pods were as follows.

2 3 3 4 5 5 5 6 7 8 8 9 9 10

Find the mean and standard deviation of the number of peas in a pod.

2 Fifteen sacks of potatoes were taken from a lorry and weighed to the nearest kilogram:

49 52 47 53 55 48 50 50 54 52 51 52 49 50 53

Calculate the mean and standard deviation of these weights.

3 Twenty-five students in a class weigh themselves in kilograms and the values are confidentially recorded. The teacher tells them that $\sum w = 1245$ and $\sum w^2 = 62\,820$. Find the mean and standard deviation of the students' weights.

4 The heights (h) of ten seedlings were measured in centimetres and calculations gave $\sum h = 85.6$ and $\sum h^2 = 742.96$.

(a) Find the mean and standard deviation of the heights of the seedlings.

(b) It was later found that one length of 8.6 cm was entered incorrectly as 6.8 cm. Find the correct mean and standard deviation of the heights.

5 Here are the midday temperatures in °C at ten weather stations scattered around the country, on two dates a week apart.

3 May (x)	15 13 16 14 17 16 12 15 17 13	$\sum x = 148, \ \sum x^2 = 2218$
10 May (y)	18 20 17 19 16 18 20 21 19 20	$\sum y = 188, \ \sum y^2 = 3556$

(a) Find the mean and standard deviation of each set of temperatures.

(b) Use the results to write a couple of sentences comparing the two data sets.

6 A van driver makes regular journeys between two towns. She can travel on the main road or go by country lanes. She notes the time taken in minutes for each journey and records it as a value of x if it was by the main road and y if it was by country lanes. After 20 journeys by the main road and 18 by country lanes she finds that $\sum x = 770$, $\sum x^2 = 32\,525$, $\sum y = 815.4$, $\sum y^2 = 37\,819.62$.

(a) Find the mean and standard deviation of the journey times by each route.

(b) Using your answer to (a), explain why the driver might prefer to go by the route with the longer mean journey time.

C Scaling and coding (answers p 125)

C1 The dot plot below shows, in white, the data set

   18 20 22 26 28 29 30 31

The standard deviation of this data set is 4.58 (to 2 d.p.).

The black dots show the same values with 20 added.

What do you think is the standard deviation of the second set of data? Give the reason for your answer.

C2 This dot plot shows the original data doubled.

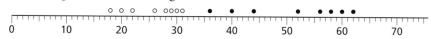

What do you think is the standard deviation of the second set of data in this case? Give the reason for your answer.

We have already seen (page 23) that if all data values are increased or decreased by the same amount, then the mean is also increased or decreased by this amount.

In symbols, if $x_1, x_2, x_3, \ldots$ become $x_1 + b, x_2 + b, x_3 + b, \ldots$
then μ becomes $\mu + b$.

So the deviation of each value from the mean is not altered by adding b.

It follows that

- If every data value is increased or decreased by the same amount, the standard deviation is unaltered.

We have also seen that if all the data values are multiplied by the same number a, then the same thing happens to the mean.

So the deviations $x_1 - \mu, x_2 - \mu, \ldots$ become $ax_1 - a\mu, ax_2 - a\mu, \ldots$

$$\text{or } a(x_1 - \mu), a(x_2 - \mu), \ldots$$

The squared deviations $(x_1 - \mu)^2, (x_2 - \mu)^2, \ldots$ become $a^2(x_1 - \mu)^2, a^2(x_2 - \mu)^2, \ldots$
In other words, the squared deviations are all multiplied by a^2.

So the variance is multiplied by a^2, so the standard deviation, which is $\sqrt{\text{variance}}$, is multiplied by a.

It follows that

- If every data value is multiplied by a, the standard deviation is also multiplied by a.

The results above can be combined into a single statement:

  If each data value x is replaced by $ax + b$, then
  the mean becomes $a\mu + b$ and the standard deviation becomes $a\sigma$.

C3 A teacher's class has 32 pupils with a mean age of 14.0 years and a standard deviation of 0.25 years.

Find the mean and standard deviation of the same 32 pupils exactly two years later.

C4 A teacher marks a test out of 40. The mean mark is 32.5 and the standard deviation is 8.4. On school reports a mark out of 200 must be given, so the teacher multiplies all the marks by 5.

What are the new mean and the new standard deviation?

C5 The midday temperature is recorded one day at several weather stations. The mean recorded temperature is 12°C and the standard deviation is 0.5°C.

For the readers of an American newspaper, temperatures are to be given in degrees Fahrenheit (°F). The formula for converting from °C to °F is

  temperature in °F = $1.8 \times$ (temperature in °C) + 32

Find the mean and standard deviation in degrees Fahrenheit.

Coding

Coding has already been used to make calculation of the mean easier.
It can also be used for calculating the standard deviation.

For example, here are the noon temperatures, in °C, recorded at eight weather stations.

18.7   19.8   19.1   20.8   18.5   19.0   18.4   20.9

The numbers are all above 18, so we could subtract 18 from each.
This leaves decimal remainders, which can be converted to whole numbers
by multiplying by 10. So a suitable coding formula would be

$y = 10 \times (\text{temperature} - 18)$

C6 (a) Use the coding formula above to code the eight temperatures.

(b) Verify that the mean of the coded data is 14.

(c) Verify that for the coded data $\sum y^2 = 2260$.

(d) Use the usual method to calculate the standard deviation of the **coded** data.

(e) By decoding, find the mean of the original data.

(f) When the data is coded using the formula above, what is the effect on the standard deviation of

  (i) subtracting 18   (ii) multiplying by 10

(g) Use the answers to (f) to find the standard deviation of the original data.

C7 The weights, in kg, of the members of a seven-a-side football team are

85   77   79   92   88   69   81

(a) Code this data using the formula $y = \text{weight in kg} - 75$.

(b) Find the mean and standard deviation of the coded data.

(c) Hence find the mean and standard deviation of the original data.

C8 The selling prices, in £000, of ten houses in a neighbourhood are

210   250   290   270   280   310   240   280   330   270

When this data is coded using the formula $y = \dfrac{\text{price in £000} - 200}{10}$

the following sums are obtained: $\sum y = 73$, $\sum y^2 = 639$.

(a) Find the mean and standard deviation of the coded data.

(b) Hence find the mean and standard deviation of the original data.

C9 The numbers of visitors to an exhibition on each of the six days it was open
are coded using the formula $y = \dfrac{\text{number of visitors} - 5000}{10}$

The coded numbers are

23   15   12   7   2   –3

(a) How many visitors were there on the last day?

(b) Find the mean and standard deviation of the numbers of visitors.

Example 3

The weights of a group of 16 animals were coded by the formula $y = 100 \times (\text{weight in kg} - 5)$.
After coding, the following sums were calculated: $\Sigma y = 92$, $\Sigma y^2 = 4570$.

Find the mean and standard deviation of the weights of the animals.

Solution

First find the mean of the coded data. Coded mean $= \dfrac{\Sigma y}{n} = \dfrac{92}{16} = 5.75$

Then find the s.d. of the coded data.

Coded s.d. $= \sqrt{\dfrac{\Sigma y^2}{n} - \text{coded mean}^2} = \sqrt{\dfrac{4570}{16} - 5.75^2} = 15.89\ldots$

To find the mean of the original data, 'undo' the coding formula.
'Subtract 5, multiply by 100' becomes 'divide by 100, add 5'.

Mean weight $= \dfrac{5.75}{100} + 5 = 5.0575 = 5.058$ (to 3 d.p.)

To find the standard deviation of the original data, note first that 'subtract 5'
in the coding formula makes no difference. 'Multiply by 100' means that the
coded standard deviation will be 100 times the original.

Standard deviation of weights $=$ coded s.d. $\div 100 = 0.159$ (to 3 d.p.)

Exercise C (answers p 125)

1 The mean weight, in kilograms, of 20 men is 84.2 kg and the standard deviation
   of their weights is 6.55 kg.

   Given that 1 kilogram = 2.2 pounds, find the mean and standard deviation of
   the weights of the men in pounds.

2 A laboratory worker measured the electrical resistance, in ohms, of 30 samples of a
   type of component. The mean was 2.8 ohms and the standard deviation was 0.85 ohms.

   It was later discovered that the measuring equipment was faulty and each reading
   had to be reduced by 10%. Find the new mean and standard deviation.

3 A teacher marked a test out of 30. The mean mark was 17.5 and the standard
   deviation was 6.1. For a school report a mark has to be given out of 100.
   The teacher decides to multiply the test marks by 3 and add 10.

   Find the mean and standard deviation of the marks out of 100.

4 In a science lesson, 16 students each measured the atmospheric pressure in millibars.
   Their readings were coded using the formula $y = \text{reading in millibars} - 1000$.
   It was found that $\Sigma y = 204$ and $\Sigma y^2 = 4204$.

   Find the mean and standard deviation of the students' readings.

5 The prices of the cars in a dealer's garage are as follows.

£3845 £3995 £4250 £4495 £4995 £5995 £6125 £6995 £7350

(a) Code this data using the formula $y = \dfrac{\text{price in £} - 3800}{5}$.

(b) Find the mean and standard deviation of the coded data.

(c) Hence find the mean and standard deviation of the car prices.

6 The times, in seconds, taken by 15 horses to finish in a race were coded by the formula $y = 10 \times (\text{time in seconds} - 80)$.

Given that $\sum y = 3499$, $\sum y^2 = 1\,020\,609$, find the mean and standard deviation of the finishing times of the horses.

7 Ten cars of the same model were timed over a 1000 m test track. The times taken, in seconds, are given below.

54.2 47.0 43.5 41.6 52.8 46.9 48.5 60.7 52.5 51.0

(a) Code this data using the formula $x = 10 \times (\text{time in seconds} - 50)$

(b) Find the mean and standard deviation of the coded data.

(c) Find the mean and standard deviation of the original data.

(d) Suppose that the original data were coded using a different formula, $y = 5 \times (\text{time in seconds} - 40)$. Write down the values of the coded mean and standard deviation in this case.

8 The trees in a wood are of two kinds, oak and beech. The heights of the 26 oak trees are measured in metres and the data is coded using the formula $u = \text{height in metres} - 15$.

(a) Given that $\sum u = 218.4$ and $\sum u^2 = 3036.8$, find the mean and standard deviation of the heights of the oak trees measured.

(b) The heights of the 19 beech trees are also measured and the results coded using the same formula. For these trees, $\sum u = 41.8$ and $\sum u^2 = 1400.87$. Find the mean and standard deviation of the heights of the beech trees measured.

(c) Compare the heights of the two kinds of tree measured.

9 In a TV antiques programme, a painting was shown to 20 members of the audience, who were asked to to estimate its value.

The estimates were coded using the formula $y = \dfrac{\text{estimate in £} - 30\,000}{500}$.

It was found that $\sum y = 56$ and $\sum y^2 = 2260$.

(a) Find the mean and standard deviation of the estimates.

The same painting was shown to 8 experts. Their estimates, in £, were

23 000 25 500 20 000 24 750 19 750 22 500 24 500 20 500

(b) Find the mean and standard deviation of the experts' estimates.

(c) Comment on the differences between the two sets of estimates.

D Working with frequency distributions (answers p 125)

In a set of data some values may be repeated several times.
The following are the numbers of visits made to a doctor in a six-month period by
a group of twenty of her patients.

        0 1 5 2 1 5 3 3 2 4 3 6 2 3 1 0 1 0 3 2

This data can be recorded in a frequency table.
To find the mean and standard deviation requires Σx_i and Σx_i^2
to be calculated from the data.

When calculating Σx_i the value 3 must be included in the sum
five times. Therefore a far quicker way to find Σx_i is to multiply
each of the values by its frequency and sum these products.

Similarly in calculating Σx_i^2 each value of x_i^2 will be included
in the sum a number of times given by its frequency.

No. of visits	Frequency
0	3
1	4
2	4
3	5
4	1
5	2
6	1
Total	20

K

If each value x_i has an associated frequency f_i, then the mean and standard
deviation can be calculated by

$$\mu = \frac{x_1 f_1 + x_2 f_2 + \ldots + x_n f_n}{n} = \frac{\Sigma x_i f_i}{n} \quad \text{and} \quad \sigma = \sqrt{\frac{\Sigma x_i^2 f_i}{n} - \mu^2}$$

The number of data values, n, is the sum of the frequencies, so $n = \Sigma f_i$.

D1 (a) For the data above, calculate the value of   (i) $\Sigma x_i f_i$ (ii) $\Sigma x_i^2 f_i$

    (b) Find the mean number of visits.

    (c) Find the standard deviation of the number of visits.

D2 This frequency table shows the numbers of eggs found in the
nests of a species of bird during a survey of a woodland area.

    (a) Find the value of n for this data.

    (b) Calculate the values of $\Sigma x_i f_i$ and $\Sigma x_i^2 f_i$.

    (c) Calculate the mean and standard deviation of the
number of eggs in a nest.

No. of eggs	Frequency
0	10
1	3
2	10
3	12
4	14
5	1

In the case of a grouped frequency table, the individual data values are not known,
only the group in which they appear.

For this reason the mean can only be estimated. The usual method is to assume
that all the data values in a group can be represented by the mid-interval value
(the value halfway along the interval).

The easiest way to find the mid-interval value is to add the two ends of the interval
and divide by 2.

D3 Use mid-interval values to estimate the mean
weight of the men whose weights are shown
in this grouped frequency table.

Weight (kg)	Mid-interval	Frequency
65–70	67.5	6
70–75		10
75–80		7
80–85		2

As before, coding can be used to simplify calculations. The next example shows how the mean and standard deviation of the data in D3 are found using coded data.

Example 4

Use the coding $y = \dfrac{\text{weight in kg} - 67.5}{5}$ to calculate the mean and standard deviation of the weights shown here.

Weight (kg)	Mid-interval	Frequency
65–70	67.5	6
70–75	72.5	10
75–80	77.5	7
80–85	82.5	2

Solution

The coded mid-interval values are 0, 1, 2, 3.

$n = \sum f = 6 + 10 + 7 + 2 = 25$

$\sum yf = (0 \times 6) + (1 \times 10) + (2 \times 7) + (3 \times 2) = 30$

$\sum y^2 f = (0^2 \times 6) + (1^2 \times 10) + (2^2 \times 7) + (3^2 \times 2) = 56$

Coded mean $= \dfrac{\sum yf}{n} = \dfrac{30}{25} = 1.2$

Coded s.d. $= \sqrt{\dfrac{\sum y^2 f}{n} - \text{mean}^2} = \sqrt{\dfrac{56}{25} - 1.2^2} = 0.8944\ldots$

Mean weight $=$ coded mean $\times 5 + 67.5 = 1.2 \times 5 + 67.5 = 73.5\,\text{kg}$

Standard deviation $=$ coded s.d. $\times 5 = 0.8944\ldots \times 5 = 4.47\,\text{kg}$ (to 2 d.p.)

The mean and standard deviation calculated from a grouped frequency table are only estimates. The assumption is that the data is reasonably evenly spread within each group. Using more groups of a smaller size will lead to better estimates.

Exercise D (answers p 125)

1 The table below shows the distribution of the lengths of phone calls from an office during the morning and afternoon.

Time (min)	Frequency Morning	Frequency Afternoon
0–15	9	26
15–20	24	35
20–25	27	16
25–30	11	2
30–35	5	0

(a) What are the mid-interval values?

(b) Use the coding $y = \dfrac{\text{mid-interval} - 7.5}{5}$ to calculate an estimate of the mean and standard deviation of lengths of morning calls and of evening calls.

(c) Use your answer to (b) to make a comparison.

2 This table shows the time it takes in minutes for students to travel to their school.

(a) Find an estimate of the mean and standard deviation of the time it takes students to get to school.

(b) What could have been done when recording the data to obtain a more accurate estimate from a grouped table?

Time taken (min)	Frequency
0–14	124
15–29	205
30–44	141
45–59	87
60–89	18

3 In a statistical investigation of the works of Charles Dickens, a student recorded the lengths of a number of sentences randomly chosen from one of his novels.

The results are shown in this table.

(a) Calculate estimates for the mean and standard deviation of the number of words per sentence in this sample. Assume that the upper limit of the last interval is 60.

(b) Give two reasons why these estimates might be inaccurate.

Number of words	Frequency
1–5	2
6–10	7
11–20	46
21–30	27
31–40	19
41–50	7
50+	2
Total	110

4 The number of shots in 50 rallies between two tennis players was recorded, both before a coaching session and then again after the coaching session. The grouped frequency table below shows the results.

Number of shots in rally	Number of rallies before coaching	after coaching
1–10	32	5
11–20	12	20
21–30	3	15
31–40	2	3
41–50	1	5
51–60	0	2
Total	50	50

(a) Estimate the mean and standard deviation of the number of shots in a rally before and after the coaching session.

(b) Comment on what the answers to (a) tell you about the effect of the coaching session.

E Skewness (answers p 126)

In any histogram, the median divides the area into two equal parts.

This diagram shows the histogram of a symmetrical distribution. The mean and the median coincide.

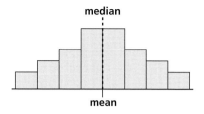

If the mean of the data in the right-hand half is further from the median than the mean of the data in the left-hand half, then the distribution has a shape that is called **positively skewed**.

The mean of the data as a whole must always be halfway between the means of the two halves. So in this case the mean of the data is greater than the median.

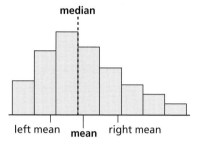

The reverse situation is shown here. The distribution is called **negatively skewed**. In this case the mean of the data as a whole is less than the median.

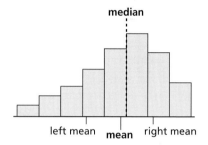

The value of (mean – median) is an indicator of skewness.

One way of arriving at a measure of skewness that can be used to compare different kinds of data set is to use

$$\frac{\text{mean} - \text{median}}{\text{standard deviation}},$$

which is a pure number without units, sometimes called a 'coefficient of skewness'.

A box plot indicates positive skewness when both right-hand sections are longer than their corresponding left-hand sections (and vice versa for negative skewness).

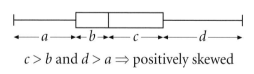

$c > b$ and $d > a \Rightarrow$ positively skewed

E1 Two exam papers were each taken by 30 candidates. Here are the marks in order.

A

36	39	40	40	41	42	43	43	44	46
49	50	51	52	54	56	59	59	60	60
61	61	62	62	65	70	71	71	73	76

$\sum x = 1636$ $\sum x^2 = 93074$

B

34	38	41	44	46	47	49	49	51	52
53	54	55	56	58	58	59	61	61	62
63	65	66	67	67	68	70	71	73	75

$\sum x = 1713$ $\sum x^2 = 101077$

(a) Find the median, mean and standard deviation of each paper.

(b) Find the 'coefficient of skewness' for each paper, defined as above.

(c) What do the values of each of the measures you have found tell you about any differences between the two papers?

F Choosing and using measures of average and spread (answers p 126)

There are two basic reasons for finding and quoting an 'average' value:
to summarise a set of data by giving a 'representative' value, or to make
comparisons. The choice of which measure to use may be guided by
features of the data or by what the result will be used for.

F1 This table shows the annual wages, in £000, of the workers
in a factory.

(a) (i) Estimate the median wage.

(ii) Estimate the mean wage.

(b) Which of the two measures do you think is more
representative of wages at this factory?

Wage (£000)	Frequency
10–20	100
20–30	80
30–40	40
40–60	35
60–80	20
80–120	5

The median wage is the wage of the 'middle-earning' worker. The mean wage
is found by adding up the wages of all the workers and sharing out the total
equally between the workers. In a pay dispute, the parties may use different
measures to justify their case.

The two commonly used measures of spread are standard deviation and
interquartile range. In cases where the data is to be related to a theoretical
model, the standard deviation (or variance) is used. In other situations
there may be reasons for preferring the interquartile range.

F2 A group of students took part in an experiment in which
they were given a geometrical puzzle to solve.
The time taken by each student was recorded.

A grouped frequency table of the results is given here.

(a) What feature of the data makes it impossible to estimate
with confidence the mean and standard deviation of the
times taken to solve the puzzle?

(b) Estimate the median and the interquartile range.

Time (s)	Frequency
0–20	6
20–40	14
40–60	25
60–80	15
80–100	10
100–120	6
> 120	4

In the puzzle-solving experiment, it is possible that timing stopped after 120 seconds,
so that any student who had not solved the puzzle by then was recorded as '> 120'.
However, even without knowing the times for these students, it is still possible
to find the median and the interquartile range.

The median and interquartile range are unaffected by extreme values at either
end of the distribution of the data. If extreme values are regarded as relatively
unimportant, then interquartile range may be a better measure of spread.

The mean and standard deviation are more 'sensitive' measures as they take into account
all the actual data values and thus give a better picture of the whole data set.

Users of statistics are sometimes guilty of choosing a measure that shows the
results they would like to be true. In practice it is best to use one or both sets
of measures but point out any limitations of the measures in the light of the data.

Measure of average	Advantages	Disadvantages
Mode	With data such as clothes sizes the mode is a useful statistic, since it is the 'most popular' size. The modal group is also useful with grouped data.	The mode is of no use with small data sets and in some cases does not give a central value. The modal group will depend on how the data was grouped initially.
Median	It is not unduly influenced by one or two extreme values or outliers.	It is insensitive as it does not use the whole data set and is governed by only a small section of the data in the middle. Calculators are difficult to program to find the median.
Mean	It uses the whole data set and thus represents every item of data. Its calculation can easily be written as a mathematical formula and calculators can easily be programmed to find it.	It can be greatly affected by a small number of outliers.

Measure of spread	Advantages	Disadvantages
Range	It shows the full extent of the spread of the data. It is easy to understand.	It is dependent only on the most extreme values.
Interquartile range	It is not unduly influenced by one or two extreme values or outliers. Useful statements can be made about a single set of data such as that 50% of the data lie within the IQR.	It is insensitive as it does not use the whole data set and is governed by two small sections of the data. Calculators are difficult to program to find the IQR.
Standard deviation and variance	They use the whole data set and thus represent every item of data. Their calculation can easily be written as a mathematical formula and calculators can easily be programmed to find them. They are useful in comparing two sets of data.	They can be greatly affected by one or two outliers. For a single set of data the standard deviation gives little useful information.

Key points

- The mean μ of a data set $x_1, x_2, x_3, \ldots, x_n$ is defined by $\mu = \dfrac{\sum x_i}{n}$. (p 22)

- The standard deviation σ of a data set $x_1, x_2, x_3, \ldots, x_n$ is defined by
  $\sigma = \sqrt{\dfrac{\sum(x_i - \mu)^2}{n}}$. A more convenient formula is $\sigma = \sqrt{\dfrac{\sum x_i^2}{n} - \mu^2}$. (pp 27–28)

- If the values of x are transformed using the formula $y = ax + b$, then the mean of y is $a\mu + b$ and the standard deviation of y is $a\sigma$. (pp 23, 30)

- If in a data set the value x_1 occurs with frequency f_1, the value x_2 with frequency f_2, and so on, then
  $$n = \sum f_i \qquad \mu = \frac{\sum x_i f_i}{n} \qquad \sigma = \sqrt{\frac{\sum x_i^2 f_i}{n} - \mu^2}$$ (p 34)

- A positively skewed distribution is one whose histogram has a shape like A below with a 'tail' to the right. A negatively skewed distribution has a shape like B.

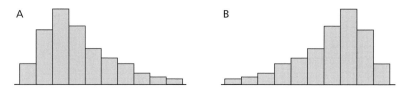

  One commonly used indicator of skewness is (mean − median) which is usually positive for a positively skewed distribution and negative for a negatively skewed distribution. The value of $\dfrac{\text{mean} - \text{median}}{\text{standard deviation}}$ is sometimes used as a coefficient of skewness to make comparisons between distributions. (p 37)

Mixed questions (answers p 126)

1 As part of their engineering course, two students have each made a pressure gauge for measuring the air pressure in tyres, balloons, and so on.
To test the gauges, each is used to measure the air pressure in a container.
This pressure has already been measured accurately and is known to be 2.4 bars.

Ten readings of this pressure are made with each gauge. The results are as follows.

Gauge A: 2.8 2.9 2.7 2.6 2.9 3.0 2.7 2.8 2.8 2.7

Gauge B: 2.7 2.5 2.8 2.2 2.4 2.3 2.7 2.9 2.1 2.4

(a) Find the mean and standard deviation of each set of readings.

(b) Suppose you had to choose one of the gauges to use. Explain why it could be better to choose A in spite of the fact that its mean reading is further from the true value.

2 The age, x years, of each of the 25 members of a games club were recorded and the following sums calculated: $\sum x = 1030$, $\sum x^2 = 44\,936$.

(a) Find the mean and standard deviation of the recorded ages.

It was discovered later that an age of 19 had been wrongly entered as 91.

(b) Find the correct values of $\sum x$ and $\sum x^2$.

(c) Find the correct mean and standard deviation of the members' ages.

3 The marks of 40 students in a test were recorded and the box plot below was drawn to show the distribution of the data.

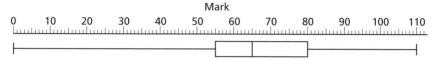

(a) Assume that the data within each section of the box plot is evenly spread, so that, for example, the 10 students in the interval 55–65 have a mean mark halfway between 55 and 65, or 60.

Estimate the mean mark of the students and show that in this case (mean – median) is negative.

(b) Estimate the mean mark for the box plot below.
Is (mean – median) positive or negative for this distribution?

(c) Comment on the skewness of each of the two distributions.

4 The table shows information about the heights of a group of 250 girls.

Minimum height	135 cm
20th percentile	149 cm
40th percentile	159 cm
60th percentile	167 cm
80th percentile	170 cm
Maximum height	174 cm

(a) How many girls have heights in the interval 135–149 cm?

(b) How many have heights in the interval 149–159 cm?

(c) Estimate the mean height of the girls.

(d) Use linear interpolation to estimate the median height.

(e) What do your answers to (c) and (d) suggest about the skewness of the distribution?

(f) Give reasons why the results in (c) and (d), and thus the suggestion in (e), may not be reliable.

Test yourself (answers p 126)

1 The value of daily sales, to the nearest £, taken at a newsagents last year are summarised in the table below.

Sales in £	No. of days
1–200	166
201–400	100
401–700	59
701–1000	30
1001–1500	5

(a) Draw a histogram to represent these data.

(b) Use interpolation to estimate the median and interquartile range of daily sales.

(c) Estimate the mean and standard deviation of these data.

The newsagent wants to compare last year's sales with other years.

(d) State whether the newsagent should use the median and the interquartile range or the mean and the standard deviation to compare daily sales. Give a reason for your answer.   Edexcel

2 Hospital records show the number of babies born in a year. The number of babies delivered by 15 male doctors is summarised by the stem-and-leaf diagram.

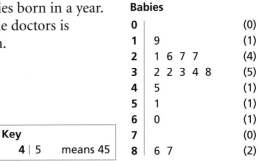

Babies

0		(0)
1	9	(1)
2	1 6 7 7	(4)
3	2 2 3 4 8	(5)
4	5	(1)
5	1	(1)
6	0	(1)
7		(0)
8	6 7	(2)

Key
4 | 5   means 45

(a) Find the median and interquartile range of these data.

(b) Given that there are no outliers, draw a box plot on graph paper to represent these data. Start your scale at the origin.

(c) Calculate the mean and standard deviation of these data.

The records also contain the number of babies delivered by 10 female doctors.

34 30 20 15 6
32 26 19 11 4

The quartiles are 11, 19.5 and 30.

(d) Using the same scale as in part (b) and on the same graph, draw a box plot for the data for the 10 female doctors.

(e) Compare and contrast the box plots for the data for male and female doctors.   Edexcel

3 Probability

In this chapter you will learn how to
- find the probabilities of combinations of events
- use conditional probabilities

A Modelling (answers p 127)

The study of probability developed quickly in the seventeenth century in connection with games of chance. Since then the ideas of probability have been applied in many areas of science, including physics and biology.

The basic ideas of probability can be explained through a simple example.

Suppose a bag contains 5 counters – 3 black (B_1, B_2, B_3) and 2 white (W_1, W_2).

You shake the bag and take out a counter without looking.
The counter you take out could be any of the five and there is no reason to think that any one counter is more likely to be taken out than any other. This is called taking a counter **at random**.

Taking a counter at random from the bag is an **experiment**. An experiment is something you do whose outcome is not known for certain.

Each of the five counters is a possible **outcome** of the experiment.
Each outcome is **equally likely**. The set of equally likely outcomes (B_1, B_2, B_3, W_1, W_2) is called the **sample space** of the experiment.

'The counter taken out is black' is a statement of something that may or may not happen when the experiment is carried out.
Something that may or may not happen is called an **event**.

The event 'the counter taken out is black' will happen if the outcome of the experiment is either B_1, B_2 or B_3. These outcomes are called **favourable** to the event.

The **probability** of an event is defined as $\dfrac{\text{number of favourable outcomes}}{\text{total number of equally likely outcomes}}$

So the probability of the event 'the counter taken out is black' is $\frac{3}{5}$.

A simple set-up like the one described above – random choice from a bag of counters – can be used to represent, or **model**, a situation in the real world.

For example, a major concern of manufacturers of appliances, such as hair dryers and electric kettles, is reliability. Some appliances are made up of hundreds of components and their reliability is difficult to model mathematically, but some understanding of the issue can be gained from simple models.

Suppose a company makes a simple appliance that consists of just two components, A and B. Every time the appliance is used, each component may work or fail. Suppose that the probability that A works is $\frac{5}{6}$ and the probability that B works is also $\frac{5}{6}$ and that the two components behave independently of each other. The appliance fails if either component fails.

A1 This situation can be modelled by rolling two dice. If either shows six, that component fails.
Carry out this experiment for long enough to estimate the reliability of the appliance, which is the proportion of times it works.

A2 A second appliance also has two components, C and D.
For each of these, the probability of working is only $\frac{1}{2}$.
However, in this appliance the components are arranged so that the appliance fails only if both components fail.
Investigate the reliability of this appliance.

In fact it is not necessary to use real dice, because the probability of failure can be calculated from the models using the methods described later in this chapter. The models are then mathematical models.

It can be shown that the reliability of the second appliance is greater than that of the first, even though the individual components are less reliable. Information like this may be of use to the company making the appliances.

Now suppose that the company finds in practice that the first appliance is not as reliable as predicted by the model. It could be that the two components are not independent of each other, but affect each other so that if one fails then the other is more likely to fail as well. It could also be that the reliability of each component decreases slightly every time it is used.

The model would then need to be altered to take account of such things.

The example above illustrates the process of **mathematical modelling**:

- Start with a situation in the real world (the reliability of an appliance).
- Decide on the type of model needed (probability model).
- Identify the quantities, called **parameters**, whose values are needed for the model (the probability of failure of each component).
- Collect the data needed to find the values of the parameters (carry out experiments with the components, or get information from available sources).
- By working mathematically with the model, answer questions and make predictions about the real world (calculate the reliability of the appliance).
- Compare the predictions with the real world by collecting appropriate data (collect data about the reliability in practice of the real appliance).
- If there is a discrepancy, improve the model (take account of the possibility that the components affect one another or that reliability decreases with use).

Modelling is important in all applications of mathematics. You will meet other examples in this book.

B Outcomes and events (answers p 127)

Some of the examples in this chapter are based on an ordinary pack of 52 cards.
The cards are split into four 'suits': clubs (♣), diamonds (♦), hearts (♥), spades (♠).
In each suit the 13 cards are: Ace, numbers 2–10, Jack (J), Queen (Q) and King (K).
The Jacks, Queens and Kings are called 'court cards' (or 'picture cards').

Let C stand for the event 'a court card is chosen'.
The number of outcomes favourable to C is denoted by n(C).

B1 What is the value of n(C)?

B2 Let D be the event 'a diamond is chosen'. What is the value of n(D)?

The events C and D can be shown in a **Venn diagram**.

Think of the rectangle as containing all the cards in the pack.
The circle labelled C contains the court cards.
The circle labelled D contains the diamonds.

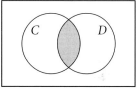

$C \cap D$ shaded

The shaded intersection of C and D contains the cards that
are both court cards and diamonds (J♦, Q♦, K♦).
This set of cards is denoted by $C \cap D$ ('C and D').
n($C \cap D$) = 3.

B3 The overlapping circles C and D divide the rectangle
into four 'compartments'. The number of outcomes
in each compartment can be written on the diagram.
What are the three missing numbers here?

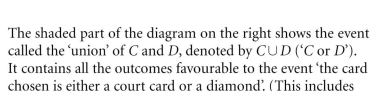

The shaded part of the diagram on the right shows the event
called the 'union' of C and D, denoted by $C \cup D$ ('C or D').
It contains all the outcomes favourable to the event 'the card
chosen is either a court card or a diamond'. (This includes
cards which are both.)

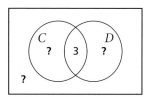

$C \cup D$ shaded

B4 What is the value of n($C \cup D$)?

The shaded part of this diagram shows the event 'the card
chosen is not a court card'. This event, called the **complement**
of C, is denoted by C'.

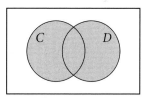

B5 What is the value of   **(a)** n(C')   **(b)** n(D')

To summarise the notation: if A and B are any two events,
A' is the event 'A does not happen',
$A \cap B$ is the event 'A and B both happen',
$A \cup B$ is the event 'either A or B (or both) happens'.

This Venn diagram shows the event C defined on the previous page, together with its complement C'.

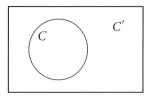

There are 52 equally likely outcomes when a card is picked at random from the pack.

The probability of C is denoted by P(C). $P(C) = \dfrac{n(C)}{52} = \dfrac{12}{52} = \dfrac{3}{13}$

D **B6** Find the value of $P(C')$.
Verify that $P(C') = 1 - P(C)$.

Use a Venn diagram or otherwise to explain why, for any event A,
$P(A') = 1 - P(A)$.

B7 The diagram shows the two events C and D defined previously.

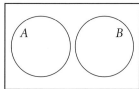

  (a) Find the value of   **(i)** $P(C \cap D)$ **(ii)** $P(C \cup D)$

  (b) Verify that $P(C \cup D) = P(C) + P(D) - P(C \cap D)$.

  (c) Use a Venn diagram to explain why, for any two events A and B,
$$P(A \cup B) = P(A) + P(B) - P(A \cap B)$$

The diagram shows two events A and B which have no outcomes in common. (In other words, A and B can't both happen together.) A and B are called **mutually exclusive events**.

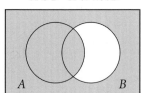

mutually exclusive events

(An example is A = 'the chosen card is a club',
B = 'the chosen card is a heart'.)

  B8 **(a)** If A and B are mutually exclusive, what is the value of $P(A \cap B)$?

     (b) What can you say about $P(A \cup B)$ when A and B are mutually exclusive?

K For any events A, B: $P(A') = 1 - P(A)$ (1)

              $P(A \cup B) = P(A) + P(B) - P(A \cap B)$ (2)

If $P(A \cap B) = 0$, then A and B are mutually exclusive and
$$P(A \cup B) = P(A) + P(B) \qquad\qquad (3)$$

The different combinations of two events A and B in a Venn diagram can be described using $\cap$ and $\cup$. For example:

$A \cap B'$ A and not B $A' \cap B$ B and not A $A' \cap B'$ not A and not B $A \cup B'$ A or not B

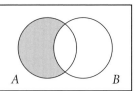
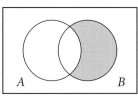
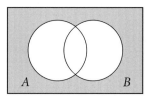
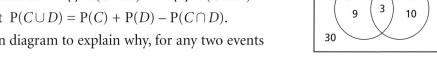

Some of the questions in exercise B below can be tackled either by using a Venn diagram or by using the three equations (1), (2), (3) on the previous page.

The next examples show the two different methods.

Example 1

There are 84 members in a sports club. 57 members play football.
48 members play basketball. 7 members play neither football nor basketball.

A member is chosen at random from the club.
What is the probability that the member chosen plays

(a) both football and basketball   **(b)** only one of the two sports

Solution

Represent the situation by a Venn diagram.

The number outside   *Add the 57 in F*   *... leaving 20 in*   *So there must be 28 in F ∩ B*
both circles is 7.   *to make 64, ...*   *B but outside F.*   *and 29 in F but not B.*

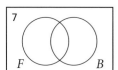   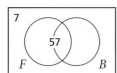   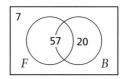   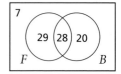

(a) P(football and basketball) = $\frac{28}{84} = \frac{1}{3}$ **(b)** P(only one sport) = $\frac{49}{84} = \frac{7}{12}$

Example 2

In a college, the proportion of students who study history is 35%. The proportion who study maths is 50%. The proportion who study neither history nor maths is 30%.
A student is chosen at random. Find the probability that the student studies

(a) either history or maths

(b) both history and maths

(c) only one of the two subjects

Solution

(a) 30% of students study neither H(istory) nor M(aths), leaving 70% that study either H or M. So $P(H \cup M) = 0.7$

(b) Use the equation $P(H \cup M) = P(H) + P(M) - P(H \cap M)$:
$$0.7 = 0.35 + 0.5 - P(H \cap M), \text{ from which } P(H \cap M) = 0.15$$

(c) P(only one of the subjects) = $P(H \cup M) - P(H \cap M)$
$$= 0.7 - 0.15 = 0.55$$

Exercise B (answers p 127)

1 In a raffle, 1000 tickets are sold, numbered from 1 to 1000. One winning ticket is picked at random. Find the probability that the winning number is

(a) a multiple of 5

(b) a multiple of 5 but not a multiple of 20

(c) a multiple of 4 or a multiple of 5

2 In a college, 50% of students study maths and 35% study science. 55% of students study either maths or science.

(a) Draw a Venn diagram to show this information.

(b) A student is picked at random. Find the probability that the student studies

(i) both maths and science (ii) only one of the two subjects

3 The events A and B are such that $P(A) = 0.65$, $P(B) = 0.6$ and $P(A \cup B) = 0.85$.

By using a Venn diagram or otherwise find

(a) $P(A')$ (b) $P(A \cap B)$ (c) $P(A \cap B')$

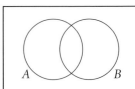

4 A box contains a collection of coloured shapes. If a shape is picked at random from the box, the probability that it is red is 0.15, the probability that it is a square is 0.36 and the probability that it is both red and square is 0.1. Find the probability that the shape is

(a) either red or square (b) red but not square (c) neither red nor square

5 The events R and S are such that $P(R) = 0.4$, $P(R \cup S) = 0.7$ and $P(R \cap S) = 0.2$.

By using a Venn diagram or otherwise find

(a) $P(R')$ (b) $P(S)$ (c) $P(R \cap S')$

6 The events A and B are such that $P(A \cap B') = 0.37$, $P(A' \cap B) = 0.41$ and $P(A' \cap B') = 0.13$. Find

(a) $P(A \cap B)$ (b) $P(A)$ (c) $P(A')$ (d) $P(A \cup B)$

7 All students at a school are required to study at least one of the three languages French, German, Spanish.
65% study French, 57% German and 36% Spanish.
40% study French and German, 13% French and Spanish.
5% study all three languages.

(a) Copy this Venn diagram and fill in the appropriate percentages.

(b) A student is picked at random. Find the probability that the student studies

(i) only French (ii) Spanish but not German

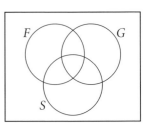

C Conditional probability (answers p 127)

Suppose a pack contains these 12 cards: ⒈ ⒉ ⒊ ⒋ ⒌ ⒍ ⒎ ⒏ ⒐ ⒑ ⒒ ⒓

A card is picked at random.

Let E be the event 'the number chosen is even'.
Let L be the event 'the number chosen is less than 6'.

The two events are shown in the Venn diagram on the right, together with the individual cards.

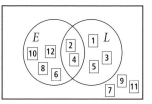

C1 Find   **(a)** $P(L)$ **(b)** $P(E)$ **(c)** $P(L \cap E)$

Suppose someone picks a card at random and tells us the number is even.

The set of equally likely outcomes is now reduced to the set for E: ⒉ ⒋ ⒍ ⒏ ⒑ ⒓

Of these cards, the only ones favourable to the event L are those in $L \cap E$: ⒉ ⒋

So the probability of L given that E has happened $= \dfrac{n(L \cap E)}{n(E)} = \dfrac{2}{6} = \dfrac{1}{3}$

The probability of L given E is written $P(L|E)$. It is called a **conditional probability**.

$P(L|E)$ can also be expressed in terms of probabilities.

Let N stand for the total number of cards in the pack. (In this example, $N = 12$.)

$$P(L|E) = \frac{n(L \cap E)}{n(E)} = \frac{\dfrac{n(L \cap E)}{N}}{\dfrac{n(E)}{N}} = \frac{P(L \cap E)}{P(E)}$$

C2 Verify that the formula $P(L|E) = \dfrac{P(L \cap E)}{P(E)}$ gives the same result ($\frac{1}{3}$) as before.

For any pair of events A, B,

$$P(B|A) = \frac{P(A \cap B)}{P(A)} \qquad (4)$$

so $P(A \cap B) = P(A)P(B|A)$ (5)

C3 (a) What does $P(E|L)$ mean, in words?   **(b)** Find the value of $P(E|L)$.

C4 Define G as the event 'the number chosen is greater than 4'. Find
    (a) $P(G|E)$ **(b)** $P(E|G)$ **(c)** $P(G|L)$ **(d)** $P(L|G)$

C5 Define M as the event 'the number chosen is a multiple of 3'.
    L is defined as before.
    (a) Draw the Venn diagram for M and L, showing each individual card.
    (b) Find   **(i)** $P(M|L)$ **(ii)** $P(L|M)$

BISHOP BURTON COLLEGE

Example 3

Dawn has a collection of photos. This table shows the number of photos in each of four categories.

	People	Places
Glossy	44	36
Matt	26	14

Dawn picks a photo at random.

(a) Given that the photo is glossy, what is the probability that it shows people?

(b) Given that the photo shows places, what is the probability that it is matt?

Solution

(a) There are $44 + 36 = 80$ glossy photos altogether. So $P(\text{people}\,|\,\text{glossy}) = \frac{44}{80} = 0.55$.

(b) There are $36 + 14 = 50$ photos of places altogether. So $P(\text{matt}\,|\,\text{places}) = \frac{14}{50} = 0.28$.

Example 4

The events A and B are such that $P(A) = 0.8$, $P(B) = 0.5$ and $P(A\,|\,B) = 0.7$.

Find   (a) $P(A \cap B)$ (b) $P(A \cup B)$ (c) $P(B\,|\,A')$

Solution

(a) *Use (5) on page 49 (with A and B reversed):* $P(A \cap B) = P(B)P(A\,|\,B) = 0.5 \times 0.7 = 0.35$

(b) *You could use equation (2) on page 46, but a Venn diagram will help here and in (c).*

$P(A \cup B) = 0.45 + 0.15 + 0.35 = 0.95$

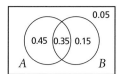

(c) *Use (4) on page 42:* $P(B\,|\,A') = \dfrac{P(A' \cap B)}{P(A')} = \dfrac{0.15}{0.2} = 0.75$

Exercise C (answers p 127)

1 A card is drawn at random from this pack.

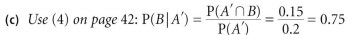

(a) Given that the card is black, what is the probability that the number on it is even?

(b) Given that the number on the card is even, what is the probability that the card is black?

2 This table shows the percentages of stamps of different types in Bharat's collection.

	UK	Foreign
Used	36%	24%
Unused	14%	26%

Bharat picks a stamp at random from the collection.

(a) What is the probability that the stamp is used?

(b) Given that the stamp is used, what is the probability that it is foreign?

(c) Given that it is a UK stamp, what is the probability that it is unused?

3 30% of the pages in a book have a picture on them. 10% have a map.
3% have both a picture and a map.

(a) Draw a Venn diagram to show this information.

A page is picked at random.

(b) Given that the page has a picture, what is the probability that it also has a map?

(c) Given that the page has a map, what is the probability that it also has a picture?

(d) What is the probability that the page has neither a map nor a picture?

(e) Given that the page does not have a picture, what is the probability that it does not have a map?

4 Each student in a college studies one and only one of the three languages French, German and Spanish. The percentage breakdown of the students by gender and by language studied is given in the table.

	French	German	Spanish
Male	30%	8%	6%
Female	21%	18%	17%

A student is picked at random.

(a) Given that the student is female, what is the probability that she studies French?

(b) Given that the student studies either German or Spanish, what is the probability that the student is male?

5 The events A and B are such that $P(A) = 0.5$, $P(B) = 0.6$ and $P(A \cup B) = 0.7$. Find

(a) $P(A \cap B)$ (b) $P(A|B)$ (c) $P(B|A)$

6 The events S and T are such that $P(S) = 0.45$, $P(T) = 0.55$ and $P(S|T') = 0.2$.

(a) Show that $P(S \cap T) = 0.36$ (b) Find $P(T|S)$

7 A market researcher asked 100 adults which of the three newspapers A, B, C they read. The results showed that 30 read A, 26 read B, 21 read C, 5 read both A and B, 7 read both B and C, 6 read both C and A and 2 read all three.

(a) Draw a Venn diagram to represent these data.

One of the adults is then selected at random. Find the probability that she reads

(b) at least one of the newspapers

(c) only A

(d) only one of the newspapers

(e) A given that she reads only one newspaper   Edexcel

D Independent events (answers p 128)

D1 Suppose you pick a card at random from this pack. $\boxed{1}\boxed{2}\boxed{3}\boxed{4}\boxed{5}\boxed{6}\boxed{7}\boxed{8}\boxed{9}\boxed{10}\boxed{11}\boxed{12}$

Define the events E and M as follows.

   E = 'the number picked is even' M = 'the number picked is a multiple of 3'

(a) Find the following probabilities.

   (i) $P(M)$ (ii) $P(E)$ (iii) $P(M|E)$ (iv) $P(E|M)$

(b) Comment on your results and what they mean.

Two events are called **independent** if knowing that one has happened makes no difference to the probability of the other.

The events M and E in question D1 are independent, because $P(M|E) = P(M)$. It is also true that $P(E|M) = P(E)$.

In general, two events B and A are independent if $P(B|A) = P(B)$.

By replacing $P(B|A)$ by the equivalent expression $\dfrac{P(A \cap B)}{P(A)}$ from equation (4) on page 49,

we can state the condition for independence as: $\dfrac{P(A \cap B)}{P(A)} = P(B)$

$$\Rightarrow \quad P(A \cap B) = P(A) \times P(B)$$

Ⓚ Two events A and B are independent when $P(A \cap B) = P(A)P(B)$ (6)

Example 5

This table shows the numbers of male and female students studying and not studying art in a college. A student is picked at random. Are the events 'the student is male' and 'the student studies art' independent?

	Male	Female
Art	27	48
Not art	83	92

Solution

There are 250 students altogether of whom 110 are male, so $P(\text{male}) = \frac{110}{250} = 0.44$.

There are 75 art students altogether, so $P(\text{art}) = \frac{75}{250} = 0.3$.

27 students are both male and study art, so $P(\text{male and art}) = \frac{27}{250} = 0.108$.

$P(\text{male}) \times P(\text{art}) = 0.44 \times 0.3 = 0.132$. This is not 0.108, so the events are not independent.

Exercise D (answers p 128)

1 This table shows the numbers of male and female students studying and not studying maths at a college. A student is chosen at random.

	Male	Female
Maths	72	58
Not maths	48	22

(a) Find the probability that the student studies maths.

(b) Given that the student is male, find the probability that the student studies maths.

(c) Show that studying maths is not independent of the gender of the student.

2 Jo and Kay are each thrown a ball. The probability that Jo catches hers is 0.3. The probability that Kay catches hers is 0.4. The two events are independent. Find the probability that

(a) Jo and Kay both catch

(b) at least one of the two girls catches

3 The events A and B are such that $P(A) = \frac{1}{2}$, $P(B) = \frac{1}{3}$ and $P(A \cup B) = \frac{2}{3}$.

(a) Find

  (i) $P(A \cap B)$ (ii) $P(A \mid B)$ (iii) $P(B \mid A)$

(b) State, with a reason, whether the events A and B are independent.

4 The events R and S are independent events such that $P(R) = 0.2$ and $P(S) = 0.5$. Find

(a) $P(R \mid S)$ (b) $P(S \mid R)$ (c) $P(R \cap S)$ (d) $P(R \cup S)$

5 The events A and B are such that $P(A) = 0.80$, $P(B) = 0.45$ and $P(A \cup B) = 0.89$. Show that A and B are independent events.

6 This Venn diagram shows two events A and B. x, y and z are the probabilities of the events represented by the corresponding parts of the diagram.

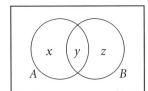

(a) Write each of these statements about A and B as an equation involving one or more of the letters x, y and z.

  (i) $P(A \cup B) = 0.84$ (ii) $P(A \mid B) = 0.6$ (iii) $P(B \mid A) = 0.75$

(b) Solve the equations in (a) and use the results to find $P(A)$.

(c) Are A and B independent? Justify your answer.

(d) Find   (i) $P(B)$ (ii) $P(A \cap B)$

7 The events S and T are such that $P(S') = 0.2$, $P(S \mid T) = 0.8$, $P(S \cup T) = 0.93$.

(a) Find $P(S \cap T)$.

(b) Find $P(T)$

(c) Show that S and T are independent.

E Tree diagrams (answers p 128)

Suppose a dice is rolled and a coin tossed. The probability of getting a six on the dice is the same, whatever happens to the coin, so the events 'six on dice' and 'head on coin' are independent.

The possible outcomes can be shown in a **tree diagram**.

Probabilities are multiplied along the branches as shown.

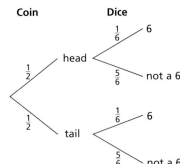

$P(\text{head and } 6) = \frac{1}{2} \times \frac{1}{6} = \frac{1}{12}$

$P(\text{head and not a } 6) = \frac{1}{2} \times \frac{5}{6} = \frac{5}{12}$

$P(\text{tail and } 6) = \frac{1}{2} \times \frac{1}{6} = \frac{1}{12}$

$P(\text{tail and not a } 6) = \frac{1}{2} \times \frac{5}{6} = \frac{5}{12}$

Where outcomes are not independent, the conditional probabilities are written on the branches.

The multiplication rule still applies because $P(A \cap B) = P(A)P(B|A)$ (equation (5) on page 49).

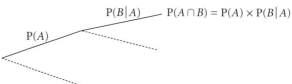

E1 An athlete has to jump over two hurdles.
The probability that he clears the first is 0.7.
If he clears the first, the probability that he clears the second is 0.6.
If he doesn't clear the first, the probability of clearing the second is 0.2.

(a) Copy and complete the tree diagram.

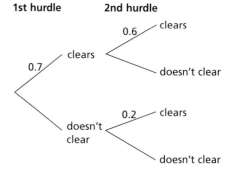

(b) What is the probability that the athlete

　(i) clears both hurdles

　(ii) clears the first but not the second

　(iii) clears the second but not the first

　(iv) clears neither hurdle

(c) Find the probability that the athlete

　(i) clears at least one hurdle

　(ii) clears exactly one hurdle

E2 A box contains 3 red and 2 green counters. A counter is taken at random from the box and is **not** replaced. Then a second counter is taken at random.

(a) What is the probability that the first counter is red?

(b) Given that the first counter is red, what is the probability that the second counter is red?

(c) Given that the first counter is green, what is the probability that the second counter is red?

(d) Draw a tree diagram. Use it to find

　(i) the probability that both counters are red

　(ii) the probability that exactly one counter is red

　(iii) the probability that both counters are green

E3 A box contains 3 dark chocolates, 2 milk chocolates and 1 white chocolate. Three chocolates are taken from the box at random, one after the other, without replacement. Find the probability that

(a) all three chocolates are dark chocolates

(b) none of the chocolates is a milk chocolate

The results obtained from a tree diagram calculation can be used to calculate a conditional probability 'in reverse'. The next example shows how.

Example 6

A trainee has two tests, A and B. The probability of passing A is 0.8.
If the trainee passes A, the probability of passing B is 0.9.
If they fail A, the probability of passing B is 0.6.

(a) Find the probability of passing B.

(b) Find the probability of passing at least one of the tests.

(c) Given that a trainee passes B, find the probability that they pass A.

Solution

(a) The tree diagram is drawn on the right.

$$P(\text{pass } B) = P(\text{pass } A \text{ and pass } B) + P(\text{fail } A \text{ and pass } B)$$

$$= 0.8 \times 0.9 + 0.2 \times 0.6 = 0.84.$$

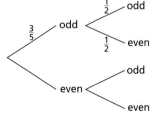

(b) 'Pass at least one' is the complement of 'fail both'.
So $P(\text{pass at least one}) = 1 - P(\text{fail both})$.

$P(\text{fail both}) = 0.2 \times 0.4 = 0.08$.
So $P(\text{pass at least one}) = 1 - 0.08 = 0.92$.

Alternatively, add $P(\text{pass } A, \text{ pass } B)$, $P(\text{pass } A, \text{ fail } B)$, $P(\text{fail } A, \text{ pass } B)$.

(c) *Use the formula for conditional probability (page 49, equation (4)).*

$$P(\text{pass } A \,|\, \text{pass } B) = \frac{P(\text{pass } A \text{ and pass } B)}{P(\text{pass } B)}$$

Use the tree diagram to find $P(\text{pass } A \text{ and } B)$. *You have already found* $P(\text{pass } B)$ *in (a).*

$P(\text{pass } A \text{ and } B) = 0.8 \times 0.9 = 0.72$. $P(\text{pass } B) = 0.84$ from (a).

So $P(\text{pass } A \,|\, \text{pass } B) = \frac{0.72}{0.84} = 0.857$ (to 3 s.f.).

Exercise E (answers p 128)

1 A pack contains cards numbered 1, 2, 3, 4, 5.
A card is picked at random and not replaced;
then another card is picked.
Copy and complete the tree diagram and find
the probability that the numbers chosen consist
of one odd and one even.

2 A pack contains six cards numbered 1 to 6.
A card is taken at random and not replaced; then a second card is taken.
Find the probability that at least one of the numbers is greater than 3.

3 A team consists of 6 girls and 4 boys. A group of 3 members of the team is picked at random. Below are two **incorrect** 'methods' of finding the probability that the chosen three consist of two girls and one boy. Say why each 'method' is wrong and then find the probability correctly.

- The probability of choosing a girl (G) is $\frac{6}{10}$ and of choosing a boy (B) is $\frac{4}{10}$.

  So the probability of GGB is $\frac{6}{10} \times \frac{6}{10} \times \frac{4}{10} = \frac{144}{1000}$.

- The probability that the first member chosen is a girl is $\frac{6}{10}$.

  If the first is a girl, that leaves 5 girls out of 9 members for the second choice and then 4 boys out of 8 members for the third. So the probability of choosing two girls and a boy is $\frac{6}{10} \times \frac{5}{9} \times \frac{4}{8} = \frac{120}{720}$.

4 In a school there are 80 teachers, 60 of whom are female. 80% of the female teachers are married. 70% of the male teachers are married.

(a) A teacher is picked at random from the staff. Using a tree diagram, find the probability that this teacher is

   (i) female and married   (ii) not married

(b) Given that the teacher picked is married, find the probability that the teacher is male.

5 Two companies, A and B, make fireworks. Experience has shown that the probability that a firework made by company A works properly when lit is 0.85. The corresponding probability for company B is 0.75.

A box contains 40 fireworks made by A and 10 made by B. A firework is taken at random from the box and lit.

(a) Draw a tree diagram to represent this situation.

(b) Find the probability that the firework picked works properly.

(c) Given that the firework does not work properly, find the probability that it was made by company B.

6 A piece of equipment contains a heating element and a warning lamp. The probability that the element overheats when the equipment is switched on is 0.1. If the element overheats, the probability that the lamp lights is 0.95. If the element does not overheat, the probability that the lamp lights is 0.2.

(a) Find the probability that the warning lamp lights when the equipment is switched on.

(b) Given that the warning lamp lights, find the probability that the element is overheating.

The method you have been using to calculate a conditional probability 'in reverse' can be expressed in symbols.

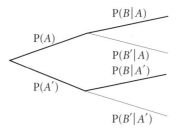

$$P(A|B) = \frac{P(A \cap B)}{P(B)}$$

$$= \frac{P(B|A)P(A)}{P(B|A)P(A) + P(B|A')P(A')}$$

Key points

- Notation: A' means 'not A'
  $A \cap B$ means 'A and B'
  $A \cup B$ means 'A or B (or both)'   (p 45)

- $P(A') = 1 - P(A)$ (p 46)

- $P(A \cup B) = P(A) + P(B) - P(A \cap B)$ (p 46)

- If A and B are mutually exclusive, then $P(A \cup B) = P(A) + P(B)$ (p 46)

- $P(B|A)$ means the conditional probability of B given A.   (p 49)

- $P(B|A) = \dfrac{P(A \cap B)}{P(A)}$ so $P(A \cap B) = P(A)\,P(B|A)$ (p 49)

- If $P(A \cap B) = P(A)P(B)$, then A and B are independent (and vice versa)   (p 52)

Mixed questions (answers p 129)

1 (a) An electrical appliance is modelled as two components,
A and B. They are connected together as shown.
The electric current flows between the points marked
● and ○ so the appliance fails if either component fails.

The probability that A fails when the appliance is switched on is 0.08 and
the probability that B fails is 0.05. The components behave independently.
Find the probability that the appliance fails when it is switched on.

(b) Another appliance contains a third component C
for which the probability of failure is 0.4.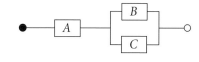
The three components are connected as shown.
As before, they behave independently.

In this case the appliance fails if either A fails or both B and C fail.
Find the probability that this appliance fails when it is switched on.

2 The events A and B are such that $P(A) = 0.7$, $P(A \cup B) = 0.88$ and $P(B|A) = 0.6$.
Show that A and B are independent.

*3 Assume that if you meet a 'random person' (for example, a total stranger at
a party) then it is equally likely that they were born on any day of the week.

(a) If you meet three strangers, what is the probability that

(i) none were born on the same day of the week as you

(ii) exactly one was born on the same day of the week as you

(b) If three strangers meet, what is the probability that no two of them were
born on the same day of the week?

Test yourself (answers p 129)

1 The events A and B are independent such that $P(A) = 0.25$ and $P(B) = 0.30$.
Find

(a) $P(A \cap B)$ **(b)** $P(A \cup B)$ **(c)** $P(A|B')$ *Edexcel*

2 The employees of a company are classified as management, administration or production.

The table shows the number employed in each category and whether or not they live close to the company or some distance away.

	Live close	Live some distance away
Management	6	14
Administration	25	10
Production	45	25

An employee is chosen at random.
Find the probability that this employee

(a) is an administrator

(b) lives close to the company, given that the employee is a manager

Of the managers, 90% are married, as are 60% of the administrators and 80% of the production employees.

(c) Construct a tree diagram containing all the probabilities.

(d) Find the probability that an employee chosen at random is married.

An employee is selected at random and found to be married.

(e) Find the probability that this employee is in production.   *Edexcel*

3 The events A and B are such that $P(A) = \frac{2}{5}$, $P(B) = \frac{1}{2}$ and $P(A|B') = \frac{4}{5}$.

(a) Find

     (i) $P(A \cap B')$ **(ii)** $P(A \cap B)$ **(iii)** $P(A \cup B)$ **(iv)** $P(A|B)$

(b) State, with a reason, whether or not A and B are

     (i) mutually exclusive   **(ii)** independent   *Edexcel*

4 For any married couple who are members of a tennis club, the probability that the husband has a degree is $\frac{3}{5}$ and the probability that the wife has a degree is $\frac{1}{2}$. The probability that the husband has a degree, given that the wife has a degree, is $\frac{11}{12}$.

A married couple is chosen at random.

(a) Show that the probability that both of them have a degree is $\frac{11}{24}$.

(b) Draw a Venn diagram to represent these data.

Find the probability that

(c) only one of them has a degree

(d) neither of them has a degree

Two married couples are chosen at random.

(e) Find the probability that only one of the two husbands and only one of the two wives have degrees.   *Edexcel*

4 Linear regression

In this chapter you will learn how to
- calculate the equation of a least squares regression line and use it to make predictions
- find a regression equation using coding of the data

A The least squares regression line (answers p 130)

In an experiment, some students let a toy car run down a ramp and measured the distance it travelled along the floor from the bottom of the ramp.
The ramp was raised to different heights above the ground and the distance travelled was measured for each height.

These are the results that they obtained.

Height (cm)	5	10	15	20	25	30	35	40	45
Distance (cm)	40	44	106	91	175	138	169	175	187

A1 Draw a scatter diagram of this data on graph paper with height on the x-axis and distance on the y-axis.
What does this suggest about the relationship between the two variables?

The relationship of interest is how the height of the ramp affects the distance the car travels along the floor. In this case the height is the **explanatory variable** as it is the height of the ramp that affects the distance travelled. The explanatory variable is usually plotted as x. In this case height is also a **controlled** variable, that is it goes up in regular steps decided by the experimenter.

The distance travelled depends on the height, so distance is the **response variable**. The response variable is usually plotted as y.

If the ramp height is fixed, at say 20 cm, and the car is released several times, it would travel a different distance each time. The distance travelled is a random variable. The height, being decided by the experimenter, is not a random variable.

A2 Until now, you have probably drawn lines of best fit 'by eye'.
(a) Draw a line of best fit 'by eye' on your scatter diagram.
(b) Find the equation of your line in the form $y = a + bx$.
(c) Find the mean of the x-values and the mean of the y-values.

The mean of the x-values is denoted by $\bar{x}$ ('x-bar') and the mean of the y-values by $\bar{y}$.

This scatter diagram shows all the points from the ramp experiment. The point $(\bar{x}, \bar{y})$ has also been plotted.

Since this point can be thought of as the 'centre' of the data, it seems reasonable that any line of best fit should pass through $(\bar{x}, \bar{y})$. This can be proved but the proof is beyond the scope of this course.

Given that the line passes through this point, we need to find the gradient (b) of the line that best fits the data.

The equation of the line will then be given by

$$(y - \bar{y}) = b(x - \bar{x})$$

or $\qquad y = bx + (\bar{y} - b\bar{x}) \quad$ where $(\bar{y} - b\bar{x})$ is the intercept.

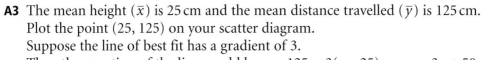

We can now investigate different values of b to see which gives the best fit.

A3 The mean height ($\bar{x}$) is 25 cm and the mean distance travelled ($\bar{y}$) is 125 cm.
Plot the point (25, 125) on your scatter diagram.
Suppose the line of best fit has a gradient of 3.
Then the equation of the line would be $y - 125 = 3(x - 25)$ or $y = 3x + 50$.
Plot this line on your graph.

In order to decide on the 'best' gradient, a method of comparison is needed. The vertical distance, d_i, can be measured from each actual point to the corresponding point predicted by the line. A line which passes closer to the points will generally have smaller values of d_i.

One method of finding the best straight line through these points is to find the gradient which minimises these deviations.

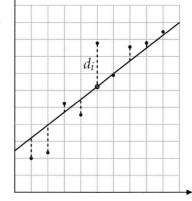

D **A4** Using a spreadsheet on a computer or graphic calculator, calculate a predicted value of y on the line $y = 3x + 50$ for each value of x in the original data set.
Hence calculate each vertical deviation d_i as (actual y – predicted y).
Calculate Σd_i for the line with gradient 3. What do you find?

A5 For each of the points in A4 calculate d_i^2 and find Σd_i^2 for the line with gradient $b = 3$.

A6 Now re-calculate Σd_i^2 for $b = 2.0, 2.5, 3.5, 4.0, 4.5$ and 5.0.
Plot a graph of the values of Σd_i^2 against b for all the values you have recorded.
What does this suggest is the value of b that minimises Σd_i^2?
Use your spreadsheet to try to find a more accurate value for b.
Compare this value with your equation in A2(b).

The line which minimises the sum of the squared deviations of the actual values from the line is called the **least squares regression line of y on x**.

The gradient b of this line is called the **regression coefficient**.

The method of finding b is given below. (It can be proved, but the proof is beyond the scope of this book.)

The data pairs are denoted by $(x_1, y_1), (x_2, y_2), \ldots$ or in general (x_i, y_i).

The number of data pairs is denoted by n.

First we define two quantities denoted by S_{xy} and S_{xx}.

$$S_{xy} = \Sigma(x_i - \bar{x})(y_i - \bar{y}) \qquad S_{xx} = \Sigma(x_i - \bar{x})^2$$

These quantities are most easily calculated using these formulae.

$$S_{xy} = \Sigma x_i y_i - \frac{(\Sigma x_i)(\Sigma y_i)}{n} \qquad S_{xx} = \Sigma x_i^2 - \frac{(\Sigma x_i)^2}{n}$$

The regression coefficient of y on x is $b = \dfrac{S_{xy}}{S_{xx}}$.

The equation of the least squares regression line is $y = a + bx$ where $a = \bar{y} - b\bar{x}$.

A7 For the car and ramp data,

(a) calculate the values of Σx_i, Σy_i, $\Sigma x_i y_i$, Σx_i^2

(b) show that $S_{xy} = 5770$ and $S_{xx} = 1500$

(c) find the value of b to three decimal places

(d) find the value of a to three decimal places, and hence show that regression equation is $y = 28.833 + 3.847x$

(e) plot the line on the scatter diagram

Often the reason for calculating a regression equation is to use it to predict values for which we have no reading. In the ramp experiment the distance the car might be expected to travel if the ramp was raised to different heights can be predicted using the regression equation.

A8 Use the regression equation to predict how far the car might be expected to travel if the ramp was raised to

(a) 17 cm   (b) 3 cm   (c) 60 cm

In A8 (a), the value of x is within the range of the observed values of x. Predicting a value within the range of the given data is called **interpolation**. If a straight line is an appropriate model then predictions by interpolation are usually reliable.

In A8 (b) and (c), however, the values of x are outside the range of the original data. Predicting in these cases is called **extrapolation**. Values predicted by extrapolation must be treated with caution. In the car and ramp experiment if the ramp is lowered beyond a certain height the car will not overcome friction and will fail to move. Similarly, as the ramp is raised higher the car may reach a maximum speed and not go beyond a certain distance.

In making predictions by extrapolation the assumption that the linear relationship continues to hold outside the observed range must be checked.

Fitting a straight line to a set of data is called fitting a **linear regression model**. Before doing this, check (for example, with a scatter diagram) that the data appears to follow a linear relationship.

Example 1

A student measures the length $y\,\mathrm{m}$ of a piece of elastic when different masses $x\,\mathrm{kg}$ are hanging on it. The results are shown in the table.

x	0.3	0.4	0.5	0.6	0.7	0.8
y	0.22	0.36	0.48	0.65	0.75	0.89

Find the equation of the regression line of y on x, giving a and b to three decimal places.

Solution

First calculate these sums. $\quad \Sigma x = 3.3 \quad \Sigma y = 3.35 \quad \Sigma x^2 = 1.99 \quad \Sigma xy = 2.077$

$$S_{xy} = \Sigma xy - \frac{(\Sigma x)(\Sigma y)}{n} = 2.077 - \frac{3.3 \times 3.35}{6} = 0.2345 \quad \textit{Do not lose accuracy by rounding.}$$

$$S_{xx} = \Sigma x^2 - \frac{(\Sigma x)^2}{n} = 1.99 - \frac{3.3^2}{6} = 0.175$$

$$b = \frac{S_{xy}}{S_{xx}} = \frac{0.2345}{0.175} = 1.340 \qquad\qquad a = \bar{y} - b\bar{x} = \frac{3.35}{6} - 1.340 \times \frac{3.3}{6} = -0.179 \text{ to 3 d.p.}$$

The regression equation is $y = -0.179 + 1.340x$.

Exercise A (answers p 130)

Give values of a and b correct to three decimal places.

1 A student drops a ball from different heights, $x\,\mathrm{m}$, above the floor and measures the height, $y\,\mathrm{m}$, to which the ball rebounds. The results are:

x	0.6	0.8	1.0	1.2	1.4	1.6	1.8	2.0	2.2	2.4
y	0.44	0.60	0.73	0.90	1.03	1.12	1.24	1.47	1.55	1.61

Given that $\Sigma x = 15$, $\Sigma y = 10.69$, $\Sigma x^2 = 25.8$, $\Sigma xy = 18.234$,

(a) find the value of

    (i) S_{xy} (ii) S_{xx} (iii) b (iv) a

(b) write down the equation of the regression line of y on x

2 A horticulturist applies different amounts of fertiliser x mg/l to ten plots of tomatoes and records the average growth y cm of the plants over a two-week period. These are the results.

x	0	5	10	15	20	25	30	35	40	45
y	13.4	15.1	21.2	22.9	25.6	26.3	28.1	30.9	31.7	30.2

(a) Draw a scatter diagram of this data.
Is a linear regression model appropriate in this case?

(b) Given that $\Sigma x = 225$, $\Sigma y = 245.4$, $\Sigma x^2 = 7125$, $\Sigma xy = 6352$,
calculate the least squares regression line of y on x in the form $y = a + bx$.

(c) Plot your regression line on the graph.

(d) Use your regression equation to predict the growth of plants to which the following amounts of fertiliser were applied.

   (i) 22 mg/l   (ii) 3 mg/l   (iii) 50 mg/l

(e) Say, with reasons, how reliable you think each of your estimates in (d) is.

3 An elastic band is hung from a hook and different weights w grams are attached to it. The length l cm of the elastic band is measured for each weight.

w	0	25	50	75	100	125	150	175	200
l	10.5	18.8	26.2	40.1	46.2	53.8	65.3	70.1	89.2

(a) Draw a scatter diagram of this data.
Is it appropriate to fit a straight line to this data?

(b) Given that $\Sigma w = 900$, $\Sigma l = 420.2$, $\Sigma w^2 = 127\,500$, $\Sigma wl = 56\,035$,
calculate the least squares regression line of length (l) on weight (w).

(c) Plot your regression line on the graph.

(d) Use your regression equation to predict the length of the elastic band if the weights attached were

   (i) 60 g   (ii) 300 g

(e) Why might the answer to (d) (ii) be unreliable?

4 The engine size s litres of ten cars with different sized petrol engines is shown in the table below together with the fuel economy f m.p.g. of each car.

s	1.0	1.1	1.3	1.5	1.6	2.0	3.0	3.3	3.5	3.6
f	47	46	44	40	39	33	25	19	23	18

(a) Explain why engine size is the explanatory variable in this case.

(b) Given that $\Sigma s = 21.9$, $\Sigma f = 334$, $\Sigma s^2 = 57.81$, $\Sigma sf = 626.2$,
find the least squares regression equation of f on s.

(c) What does the regression equation predict for the fuel economy of a 5.0 litre engine? Why is this prediction unreliable?

B Explanatory variables

In the examples in section A, the explanatory variable was controlled by the experimenter. In many cases it may not be possible to control the explanatory variable. For example, someone looking at how the temperature affects the sales of ice cream cannot choose the temperature at a given time but must work with the values that happen to occur.

This data shows the temperature ($t°C$) at midday in a seaside resort on various days one summer and the number n of ice creams sold at a seafront kiosk.

t	25	26	16	23	24	18	21	18	19	28
n	305	373	77	162	316	132	184	148	178	402

In this case, it is clearly the temperature which affects the ice cream sales, not the other way round. Temperature is therefore the explanatory variable. Ice cream sales is the response variable.

As shown in the previous section, a regression line is often used to predict a value for the response variable when the value of the explanatory variable is known. The choice of explanatory and response variables will depend on which of the variables the experimenter wants to predict.

For example, in criminal or archaeological investigations it sometimes happens that a single human bone, say a thigh bone, is found. Police or archaeologists may want to predict a person's height from the length of the bone.

In this case, bone length is taken as the explanatory variable and height as the response variable, since it is the height that is being predicted. Extensive data on heights and bone lengths has been collected. The regression line of height on bone length from this data is used to estimate height for a given bone length.

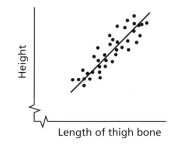

Length of thigh bone

Interpreting the intercept and gradient

In an equation of the form $y = a + bx$, a represents the **intercept** on the y-axis, that is, the value of y when $x = 0$.

The example on the right comes from an experiment in which the pressure of a gas was measured at various temperatures. The intercept a represents the value given by the regression line for the pressure at $0°C$.
The gradient b gives the increase in pressure resulting from each $1°C$ rise in temperature.

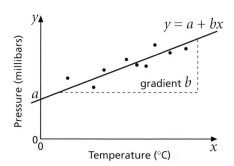

Exercise B (answers p 131)

1 (a) Find the equation of the regression line for the ice cream data opposite.
(You may use $\Sigma t = 218$, $\Sigma n = 2277$, $\Sigma t^2 = 4896$, $\Sigma tn = 53\,407$.)

(b) Use the equation to predict the sales when the midday temperature is 20 °C.

(c) What is the significance of the gradient b in this case?

2 A travelling salesman wants to be able to predict his journey time t hours to clients from the distance d miles. He records the distances he travels to eleven clients and his journey times.

d	65	137	257	84	105	346	124	157	201	98	132
t	2	2.5	6	2.25	3	7.75	3.25	3.75	4.5	2.75	3.5

(a) Which variable, distance or time, is the explanatory variable and which the response variable in this case?

(b) Plot this data on a scatter diagram and check that a linear model is suitable.

(c) Calculate the least squares regression line of t on d and plot this on the scatter diagram.

(d) What is the significance of the value of the intercept a in this case?

(e) What is the significance of the gradient b?

(f) Use the regression equation to predict the time taken for a journey of

(i) 180 miles **(ii)** 50 miles **(iii)** 420 miles

(g) Which of these predictions are likely to be reliable?
Explain why the other prediction(s) may not be reliable.

3 Atmospheric pressure is often a good indicator of weather conditions to come.
A meteorologist is interested in the possibility of predicting the maximum wind speed s km/h in an approaching tropical storm from the lowest atmospheric pressure p millibars before the storm is expected to start.
Here is data collected from seven recent storms in an area.

p	1003	976	990	935	985	931	954
s	66	160	105	230	128	242	210

(a) Plot this data on a scatter diagram and check that a linear model is suitable.

(b) Calculate the least squares regression line for predicting wind speed given lowest atmospheric pressure.
(You may use $\Sigma p = 6774$, $\Sigma s = 1141$, $\Sigma p^2 = 6\,560\,012$, $\Sigma ps = 1\,093\,080$.)

(c) What does the value of the gradient b tell you in this case?

(d) Use the regression equation to predict the maximum wind speed in an approaching storm when the lowest atmospheric pressure beforehand is

(i) 900 millibars **(ii)** 1200 millibars **(iii)** 950 millibars

(e) Which of these predictions do you think is most reliable?
Explain why the other predictions may not be so reliable.

C Coding (answers p 131)

In chapter 2 we saw how the coding of variables can make calculation of a mean, variance or standard deviation easier.

The same idea can be used to simplify the calculations involved in finding a regression equation.

Here again is the data from example 1 on page 62.

x	0.3	0.4	0.5	0.6	0.7	0.8
y	0.22	0.36	0.48	0.65	0.75	0.89

To get rid of the decimals and then make the numbers smaller, the values of x could be multiplied by 10 and then reduced by 3.
So if the new variable is called u, then

$$u = 10x - 3$$

Similarly, the values of y could be transformed by multiplying by 100 and subtracting 22.
So if v is the new variable, then

$$v = 100y - 22$$

In terms of u and v the data table looks like this.

u	0	1	2	3	4	5
v	0	14	26	43	53	67

For this **coded** data, $\Sigma u = 15$, $\Sigma v = 203$, $\Sigma u^2 = 55$, $\Sigma uv = 742$.

C1 (a) Find the values of S_{uv} and S_{uu} and hence find the regression equation for v on u.

(b) Rewrite the regression equation, replacing u by $10x - 3$ and v by $100y - 22$.
Compare the result with the answer to example 1 (page 62).

K The process of finding a regression equation by coding can be summarised like this:

- Replace the original variables x and y by new variables u and v defined in terms of x and y.
- Find the regression equation of v on u.
- Replace u and v in this equation by equivalent expressions in terms of x and y.

C2 Find the equation of the regression line of y on x for the data given here, by using the coding

$$u = 0.1x - 40 \qquad v = 10y - 30$$

x	410	430	450	470	490	510
y	3.2	3.8	4.7	5.1	5.6	6.5

Example 2

A teacher gives his students a test before an exam. He thinks the test score T is a good predictor of a student's exam mark E. He codes the results for 20 students using the coding $p = T - 10$ and $q = 0.2E - 10$.

For these 20 students, $\Sigma p = 38$, $\Sigma q = 9.2$, $\Sigma p^2 = 402$, $\Sigma pq = 176.4$.

(a) Find the equation of the regression line of q on p.

(b) Find the equation of the regression line of E on T.

(c) Use the regression equation to predict the exam mark of a student who scores 10 in the test.

Solution

(a) $S_{pq} = 176.4 - \dfrac{38 \times 9.2}{20} = 158.92 \qquad S_{pp} = 402 - \dfrac{38^2}{20} = 329.8$

$b = \dfrac{S_{pq}}{S_{pp}} = \dfrac{158.92}{329.8} = 0.481\,87$ (to 5 d.p.) *This number is used later, so don't round it too much.*

$a = \bar{p} - b\bar{q} = \dfrac{9.2}{20} - 0.481\,87 \times \dfrac{38}{20} = -0.455\,55$ (to 5 d.p.)

The regression equation is $q = -0.455\,55 + 0.481\,87p$.

(b) Replace p by $T - 10$ and q by $0.2E - 10$.

The equation becomes $0.2E - 10 = -0.455\,55 + 0.481\,87(T - 10)$

$$\Rightarrow \quad 0.2E = 10 - 0.455\,55 + 0.481\,87T - 4.8187$$

$$\Rightarrow \qquad E = 23.629 + 2.409T \text{ (to 3 d.p.)}$$

(c) If $T = 10$, the predicted value of E is $23.629 + 2.409 \times 10 = 47.719$
(48 to the nearest integer).

Exercise C (answers p 131)

1 This table gives the engine size (e litres) and the top speed (s m.p.h.) of a range of saloon cars.

e	1.3	1.5	1.6	1.8	2.0	2.5	3.0	3.3	3.5	3.6
s	102	106	117	121	137	144	149	159	174	181

(a) Explain why e is the explanatory variable in this case.

(b) Using the coding $x = 10e - 13$ and $y = s - 100$, make a table of values of x and y.

(c) Draw a scatter diagram showing pairs of values of x and y.

(d) Does the scatter diagram suggest that a linear model is appropriate?

(e) Find the equation of the regression line of y on x.

(f) Hence find the equation of the regression line of s on e.

2 An estate agent recorded the floor area, $f\text{m}^2$, of each of twelve recently sold houses in an area, together with the price, p thousand pounds, of each house. The coding $x = 0.1f - 25$ and $y = 0.1p - 10$ was used to produce this table:

x	2	3	6	7	8	11	12	16	18	21	23	27
y	1	5	4	7	5	7	9	8	7	13	14	18

(a) Draw a scatter diagram showing pairs of values of x and y.

(b) Does the scatter diagram suggest that a linear model is appropriate?

(c) Given that $\Sigma x = 154$, $\Sigma y = 98$, $\Sigma x^2 = 2706$, $\Sigma xy = 1650$, find the equation of the regression line of y on x.

(d) Find the equation of the regression line of p on f.

3 A student has made an electronic thermometer.
She tests the accuracy of her thermometer by putting it in beakers of water whose temperature, $x°C$, has been measured by another highly accurate thermometer. She records the reading $y°C$ on her thermometer for ten values of x lying in the interval $20 \leq x \leq 80$.
She codes her results so that $u = x - 50$, $v = y - 50$.

(a) Given that $\sum u = 6$, $\sum v = 17$, $\sum u^2 = 3570$, $\sum uv = 4057$, find the equation of the regression line of v on u.

(b) Hence find the equation of the regression line of y on x in the form $y = a + bx$.

(c) What does the value of a represent?

(d) Explain why it would be inadvisable to use the regression equation to predict what the student's thermometer would read for water at $100°C$.

Key points

- The linear regression equation is the equation of the line which best fits a set of data where there is an approximate linear relationship.
The least squares regression equation of y on x for a given set of data is given by

$$y = a + bx, \quad \text{where} \quad b = \frac{S_{xy}}{S_{xx}} = \frac{\sum(x_i - \bar{x})(y_i - \bar{y})}{\sum(x_i - \bar{x})^2} = \frac{\sum x_i y_i - \dfrac{\sum x_i \sum y_i}{n}}{\sum x_i^2 - \dfrac{(\sum x_i)^2}{n}}$$

and $\quad a = \bar{y} - b\bar{x}.$ (p 61)

- If the original variables x and y are coded by new variables u and v, then the regression equation of v on u can be converted into the regression equation for y on x by replacing u and v by the corresponding expressions containing x and y. (p 66)

Test yourself (answers p 132)

1 The heights of twelve girls were measured at the age of 8 (height x cm) and again at the age of 18 (height y cm). This table shows the results.

x	123	148	132	145	141	138	131	138	123	131	144	129
y	155	169	165	169	166	169	165	165	157	159	174	161

$\sum x = 1623$, $\sum y = 1974$, $\sum x^2 = 220\,279$, $\sum xy = 267\,440$

(a) Plot this data on a scatter diagram and check that a linear model is suitable.

(b) Taking x as the explanatory variable, calculate the least squares regression equation of y on x.

(c) Use your equation to predict the height at age 18 of a girl who is 150 cm tall at age 8. Do you think this is a reliable estimate? If not, why not?

2 The chief executive of Rex cars wants to investigate the relationship between the number of new car sales and the amount of money spent on advertising. She collects data from company records on the number of new car sales, c, and the cost of advertising each year, p (£000). The data are shown in the table below.

Year	No of new car sales c	Cost of advertising (£000) p
1990	4240	120
1991	4380	126
1992	4420	132
1993	4440	134
1994	4430	137
1995	4520	144
1996	4590	148
1997	4660	150
1998	4700	153
1999	4790	158

(a) Using the coding $x = (p - 100)$ and $y = \frac{1}{10}(c - 4000)$, draw a scatter diagram to represent these data. Explain why x is the explanatory variable.

(b) Find the equation of the least squares regression line of y on x.
   (Use $\Sigma x = 402$, $\Sigma y = 517$, $\Sigma x^2 = 17\,538$ and $\Sigma xy = 22\,611$.)

(c) Deduce the equation of the least squares regression line of c on p in the form $c = a + bp$.

(d) Interpret the value of a.

(e) Predict the number of extra new car sales for an increase of £2000 in the advertising budget. Comment on the validity of your answer.

Edexcel

3 A drilling machine can run at various speeds, but in general the higher the speed the sooner the drill needs to be replaced. Over several months, 15 pairs of observations relating to speed, s revolutions per minute, and life of a drill, h hours, are collected.

For convenience the data are coded so that $x = s - 20$ and $y = h - 100$ and the following summations obtained.

$\Sigma x = 143$, $\Sigma y = 391$, $\Sigma x^2 = 2413$, $\Sigma y^2 = 22\,441$, $\Sigma xy = 484$

(a) Find the equation of the regression line of h on s.

(b) Interpret the slope of your regression line.

(c) Estimate the life of a drill revolving at 30 revolutions per minute.

5 Correlation

In this chapter you will learn
- how to measure and interpret correlation
- about the effects of scaling data on correlation

A Measuring correlation (answers p 133)

In many areas of interest, statisticians are concerned about whether there is a connection between two random variables and how strong that connection is. For example, we might expect a connection between weight and waist size but not between shoe size and IQ. This chapter is about how we can measure the strength of any such connections.

Here are four sets of data.

Set 1: snails

This table gives the foot area and mass of 15 snails of the South American species *Biomphalaria glabrate*.

Foot area (mm²)	20	16	35	25	20	7	13	7	3	10	4	1	35	24	38
Mass (g)	0.64	0.21	0.85	0.53	0.18	0.06	0.20	0.07	0.01	0.05	0.02	0.01	0.81	0.38	0.61

Set 2: coins

This table shows the age and mass of ten 2p coins.

Age (years)	7	12	19	16	18	28	12	10	13	19
Mass (g)	7.21	7.34	6.84	7.25	7.24	6.93	7.13	7.33	7.15	7.12

Set 3: reactions

Eleven surgeons injected themselves with a drug to change their heart rate. They then measured their heart rates and used a computer test to measure their reaction times. These are the results.

Heart rate (b.p.m.)	134	133	132	123	118	110	98	90	84	80	80
Reaction time (ms)	438	438	467	505	531	557	541	562	591	603	617

Set 4: blood pressure

A group of 20 students weighed themselves and measured their systolic blood pressure (in millimetres of mercury) with an electronic monitor.
This is what they found.

Weight (kg)	60	45	50	37	70	67	55	41	48	38
Blood pressure (mmHg)	141	116	132	114	109	92	95	107	98	97
	59	48	52	38	49	44	43	59	50	40
	98	85	115	104	163	153	86	122	106	97

A1 Draw a scatter diagram for each of the four sets of data. You may find a spreadsheet or a graph plotter useful for this.

What do the graphs tell you about any connection between the two variables in each set of data?

Data that consists of pairs of values of two random variables is called **bivariate data**.

When investigating the connection between two variables we examine whether there tends to be a linear relationship. When there is, the two variables are said to be **correlated**.

To judge how strongly a particular pair of variables is correlated, a suitable numerical measure is necessary. Consider the following scatter diagram, where the plotted points are approximately in a straight line.

Dotted lines for $\bar{x}$ and $\bar{y}$ have been drawn.
They divide the diagram into four 'quadrants' A, B, C, D.

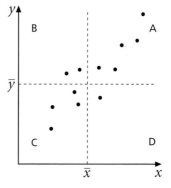

A2 If a point (x, y) is in quadrant A, what is the sign of

(a) $x - \bar{x}$ (the deviation of x from the mean)

(b) $y - \bar{y}$ (the deviation of y from the mean)

(c) $(x - \bar{x})(y - \bar{y})$ (the product of the deviations)

A3 What sign is the product of the deviations for each of the quadrants B, C and D?

A4 If the product of the deviations is found for every point on a scatter diagram and summed to give $\sum(x_i - \bar{x})(y_i - \bar{y})$, what can you say about this sum in each of these cases?

(a) When all of the points lie in quadrants A and C and the points approximate to a straight line with a positive gradient

(b) When all of the points lie in quadrants B and D and the points approximate to a straight line with a negative gradient

(c) When the points are spread evenly over all four quadrants

The quantity $\sum(x_i - \bar{x})(y_i - \bar{y})$ has been used before, in chapter 4.
It is denoted by S_{xy}.

The sign of S_{xy} tells us what type of correlation there is between x and y:

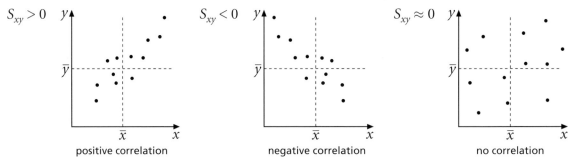

$S_{xy} > 0$	$S_{xy} < 0$	$S_{xy} \approx 0$
positive correlation	negative correlation	no correlation

Another quantity you met in chapter 4 is $S_{xx} = \sum(x_i - \bar{x})^2$.

A third quantity that you will need is defined in a similar way: $S_{yy} = \sum(y_i - \bar{y})^2$.

The English statistician Karl Pearson (1857–1936) found that the quantity $r = \dfrac{S_{xy}}{\sqrt{S_{xx}S_{yy}}}$

is a measure of correlation that does not involve the size of the data set and is independent of the units in which each variable is measured.

$r = \dfrac{S_{xy}}{\sqrt{S_{xx}S_{yy}}}$ is called the **product moment correlation coefficient** (p.m.c.c.).

The value of r always lies in the interval $-1 \le r \le 1$.

$r = 1$ corresponds to perfect positive correlation.

$r = -1$ corresponds to perfect negative correlation.

When $r = 0$, the two variables are uncorrelated.

The three quantities in the definition of r can be calculated using more convenient formulae as follows:

$$S_{xy} = \sum xy - \frac{(\sum x)(\sum y)}{n} \qquad S_{xx} = \sum x^2 - \frac{(\sum x)^2}{n} \qquad S_{yy} = \sum y^2 - \frac{(\sum y)^2}{n}$$

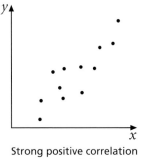

Strong positive correlation
$r \approx 0.8$

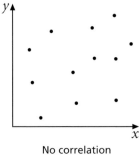

No correlation
$r \approx 0$

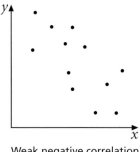

Weak negative correlation
$r \approx -0.5$

Example 1

Twelve cigarettes were sampled from a range of brands and their tar content, x mg, and nicotine content, y mg, were measured. This table shows the results.

x	16	8	4.1	15	8.8	12.4	16.6	14.9	13.7	15.1	11.4	17
y	1.06	0.67	0.40	1.04	0.76	0.95	1.12	1.02	1.01	0.90	0.78	1.26

$\sum x = 153$, $\sum y = 10.97$, $\sum x^2 = 2125.24$, $\sum y^2 = 10.6151$, $\sum xy = 149.557$

(a) Calculate the product moment correlation coefficient for this data.

(b) What does this tell you about the amount of tar and nicotine in these cigarettes?

Solution

(a) $S_{xy} = \sum xy - \dfrac{(\sum x)(\sum y)}{n} = 149.557 - \dfrac{153 \times 10.97}{12} = 9.6895$

$S_{xx} = \sum x^2 - \dfrac{(\sum x)^2}{n} = 2125.24 - \dfrac{153^2}{12} = 174.49$

$S_{yy} = \sum y^2 - \dfrac{(\sum y)^2}{n} = 10.6151 - \dfrac{10.97^2}{12} = 0.58669\ldots$

$r = \dfrac{S_{xy}}{\sqrt{S_{xx}S_{yy}}} = \dfrac{9.6895}{\sqrt{174.49 \times 0.58669}} = 0.958$ (to 3 d.p.)

(b) There is a strong positive correlation. High tar cigarettes tend to have high nicotine content.

Exercise A (answers p 133)

1 A group of students were asked to push a ball through a maze while looking in a mirror. Each student completed the maze first with their dominant hand (the hand they wrote with) and then with their other hand. The time taken using each hand was recorded as x seconds (dominant) and y seconds (other).

Student	A	B	C	D	E	F	G	H	I	J
x	76	45	32	85	79	105	143	108	56	74
y	113	52	30	78	100	141	181	98	78	105

$\sum x = 803$, $\sum y = 976$, $\sum x^2 = 74041$, $\sum y^2 = 111812$, $\sum xy = 89828$

Calculate the product moment correlation coefficient between the times taken for the two hands and comment on the result.

2 A family records for several days in March the midday temperature outside, $t°C$, and the number n of units of electricity they used that day.

t	7.4	12.3	9.6	9.0	8.7	14.7	18.2	11.3	10.4	9.3
n	48	34	42	45	44	36	34	38	48	45

$\Sigma t = 110.9,\ \Sigma n = 414,\ \Sigma t^2 = 1324.57,\ \Sigma n^2 = 17\,410,\ \Sigma tn = 4459.5$

(a) Calculate the p.m.c.c. between t and n.

(b) The family believes that on warmer days they use less electricity. Does the result in (a) support this hypothesis?

B Scaling and coding

The graphs below show a set of data, the same set of data with the y-values doubled, and the original data with 5 added to each of the x-values.

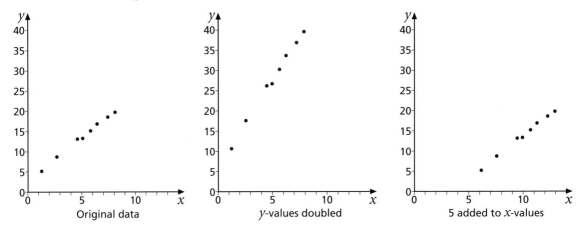

Although the position of the points in relation to the axes is different in each case, the relative spacing between the points is unchanged.

A linear transformation of either variable (for example x becomes $3x + 5$, or y becomes $\frac{1}{2}y - 10$) does not affect the correlation between x and y.

So coding does not alter the value of the correlation coefficient.

Example 2

20 trainees each did two tasks. The times taken, p s (first task) and q s (second task), were coded by $x = 10(p - 15)$ and $y = 10(q - 20)$, and the following sums calculated.

$\Sigma x = 10,\ \Sigma y = -5,\ \Sigma x^2 = 288,\ \Sigma y^2 = 385,\ \Sigma xy = -163$

Calculate the product moment correlation coefficient between p and q.

Solution

Coding does not affect the correlation, so the p.m.c.c. between p and q is equal to that between x and y. The calculation is done as in example 1 and leads to $r = -0.487$.

Exercise B (answers p 134)

1 Two people, A and B, are asked to judge the photos entered for a competition.
They are asked to give points for composition, interest, technical quality,
and so on, and to give each photo a score out of 50.
The scores they give for each entry are shown in the table below, where
a stands for the score given by A and b for the score given by B.

Entry no.	1	2	3	4	5	6	7	8	9	10	11	12	13	14	15
a	21	32	33	39	29	42	35	43	29	40	37	33	31	26	25
b	29	38	40	45	36	44	41	40	37	39	42	42	40	37	34

(a) Code this data using $x = a - 30$ and $y = b - 40$.

(b) Calculate Σx, Σy, Σx^2, Σy^2, and Σxy.

(c) Calculate the values of $\bar{x}$ and $\bar{y}$. What does the difference between these
values tell you about the judges' scores?

(d) Calculate S_{xx}, S_{yy} and S_{xy}.

(e) Find, correct to 3 significant figures, the value of the product moment
correlation coefficient between x and y.

(f) (i) Write down the value of the product moment correlation coefficient
between a and b.

(ii) Interpret the value of this correlation coefficient.

(g) Because judge A gave, on average, lower scores than B, it is decided to
add 3 to judge A's scores before announcing the marks.
Without doing any further calculation, say what the effect of this will be
on the the value of the correlation coefficient between the judges' scores.

2 A student collected information from advertisements in local papers about
the ages and prices of a particular model of car.
Here is the data for the sample he collected.

Age (years)	4	8	6	3	6	4	2	5	6	10
Price (£)	3600	1600	1000	3300	2400	4900	5500	2100	1000	900

If x = age in years and $y = \dfrac{\text{price in £}}{100}$, the following summations are found:

$\Sigma x = 54$, $\Sigma y = 263$, $\Sigma x^2 = 342$, $\Sigma y^2 = 9365$, $\Sigma xy = 1136$

(a) Calculate the value of the product moment correlation coefficient
between x and y.

(b) What is the value of the correlation coefficient between the ages and
the prices of the cars in the sample?

(c) What does the value of the correlation coefficient tell you about
the relationship between age and price for this sample of cars?

C Interpreting correlation (answers p 134)

You have probably heard the claim 'You can prove anything with statistics'. It is of course untrue: statistics never aims to prove anything but may provide evidence to support a particular theory. However, correlation is often used in inappropriate ways to 'support' claims.

A student carries out a survey of students in her school. To get a representative sample she chooses 5 students from each year group from year 7 to year 13. She records a number of variables for each student.

She draws this scatter diagram of heights and scores in a general knowledge quiz. The p.m.c.c. for this data is 0.885.

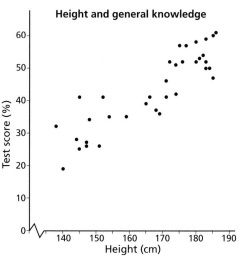

Height and general knowledge

D **C1** Does this suggest that being taller makes you better at general knowledge?

This is a common misuse of correlation. A strong correlation does not mean that one variable is the 'cause' of a second variable. A high positive correlation simply says that high values of one variable occur with high values of the other variable, and low with low. Cases such as this are referred to as **spurious** correlation.

In many cases the apparent link may be the effect of a third variable, as in the example above, where both variables are linked to age, which is likely to be the 'cause' of both variables. Older students are likely to be taller and to have better general knowledge.

There are other circumstances where an apparent correlation is due to something unusual in the data. The next question is about one such case.

C2 This data set shows the heights, h cm, and the weights, w kg, of a group of year 7 pupils together with their teacher.

x	147	154	156	161	150	163	160	158	157	183
y	45	38	59	48	37	60	59	44	45	98

$\sum x = 1589$, $\sum y = 533$, $\sum x^2 = 253\,353$, $\sum y^2 = 31\,269$, $\sum xy = 86\,120$

(a) Calculate the p.m.c.c. between x and y.

(b) The final pair are the height and weight of the teacher. Recalculate the p.m.c.c. without this data pair.

(c) Comment on the differences between the values in (a) and (b).

One or two outliers can have a dramatic effect on a correlation, either to exaggerate a strong correlation or to make an otherwise strong correlation appear weak.

In some cases a correlation may exist in a whole population but not within a subgroup of it (or vice versa). A student looking for a correlation between leg lengths and running speed collected data from members of her athletics club. She was disappointed to find a very weak correlation in the club members. However, it is still possible that a correlation may exist in the population as a whole.

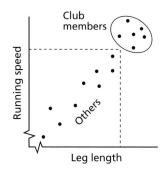

The p.m.c.c. is an appropriate measure only where the relationship between two random variables is **linear**.

The data in this graph gives a correlation coefficient of −0.1 yet it fits a non-linear relationship closely.

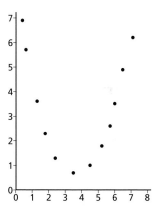

Exercise C (answers p 134)

1 Ten students measured their reaction times using their left hand (x milliseconds) and then using their right hand (y milliseconds). The results were as follows.

Student	A	B	C	D	E	F	G	H	I	J
x	15.4	18.7	23.4	19.2	22.5	25.4	20.9	16.4	21.1	19.7
y	19.6	13.2	19.4	15.3	18.6	20.9	17.6	20.3	17.2	14.8

$\Sigma x = 202.7$, $\Sigma y = 176.9$, $\Sigma x^2 = 4193.53$, $\Sigma y^2 = 3188.35$, $\Sigma xy = 3601$

(a) Calculate the p.m.c.c. between x and y for these ten students.

(b) Draw a scatter diagram to show the data.

(c) Two of the students in this experiment were left-handed. Which two do you think they were?

(d) Calculate the p.m.c.c. for the eight students who are right-handed.

(e) Comment on the values you obtained for the p.m.c.c. in (a) and (d).

2 The number of people who visited the cinema the previous week in a sample of towns in the UK was recorded. A researcher calculated the correlation between this variable and the numbers of crimes in the towns.
The p.m.c.c. obtained was 0.84.

A campaigner against violent films claimed that this was evidence that going to the cinema encouraged people to commit crimes.
Say, with reasons, whether the survey supports this point of view.

3 The maximum daily outside temperature, $x°C$, and the amount of electricity, y units, used by an office air-conditioning system were recorded as follows:

x	18.2	8.9	28.2	29.6	16.1	26.7	20.4	21.0	5.4	23.4	12.4	15.5
y	4.3	13.2	12.7	13.5	7.6	9.6	5.1	6.3	15.8	7.8	11.1	9.1

$\Sigma x = 225.8$, $\Sigma y = 116.1$, $\Sigma x^2 = 4881.84$, $\Sigma y^2 = 1268.39$, $\Sigma xy = 2115.03$

(a) Calculate the p.m.c.c. between temperature and units of electricity used. What does this suggest about the link between the temperature and the amount of electricity used?

(b) Draw a scatter diagram of this data.

(c) Explain why the p.m.c.c. may not be a good measure of the correlation in this case.

D Correlation and regression

In chapter 4, you saw how a least squares regression line may be used to predict the value of one variable (the response variable) from the value of the other (the explanatory variable). However, before trying to find the regression line, it is important to check that a linear model is appropriate. A scatter diagram can be used for this purpose.

If the two variables involved are both random variables, for example the heights and weights of a sample of children, you can calculate the product moment correlation coefficient as a way of checking whether there is enough evidence of a linear relationship to make the regression line worth finding.

If the correlation between the values of the two random variables is close to 1 or −1, then this is strong evidence of a linear relationship. In this case it is clearly reasonable to find the least squares regression line and use it to predict values of the response variable (within the range of the data).

The strength of correlation needed to make it reasonable to fit a linear model depends on how many pairs of values there are in the data. As a general rule, for a sample of 10 data pairs r should be greater than 0.55 or less than −0.55.

For 20 data pairs, $r > 0.38$ or $r < −0.38$ is sufficient evidence of a linear relationship.

The stronger the correlation, the better the fit of the linear model. The closer r is to 1 or −1, the more accurate are values predicted from the regression line.

1 A manager records the number, n, of orders received through the post each day and the time taken, t minutes, by office workers to enter each order on the computer.

n	52	24	40	53	42	56	79	36	77	51
t	342	179	397	460	419	496	664	286	640	435

$\Sigma n = 510$, $\Sigma t = 4318$, $\Sigma n^2 = 28\,656$, $\Sigma t^2 = 2\,061\,308$, $\Sigma nt = 241\,931$

(a) Find the p.m.c.c. Does this suggest a linear relationship between t and n?

(b) Taking n as the explanatory variable, find the least squares regression equation of t on n, in the form $t = a + bn$.

(c) Use the regression equation to predict the time taken to enter 70 orders.

2 Bleep tests are used to measure people's fitness. A higher score means a higher level of fitness. The pulse rate, p beats per minute, and bleep score, s, for 12 people were recorded and coded using $x = p - 60$ and $y = 10s - 50$.

x	0	−6	9	−1	5	8	30	19	28	20	36	23
y	55	62	38	−7	50	44	8	8	3	20	−14	3

$\Sigma x = 171$, $\Sigma y = 270$, $\Sigma x^2 = 4477$, $\Sigma y^2 = 13\,540$, $\Sigma xy = 1020$

(a) Find the product moment correlation coefficient between x and y.

(b) Write down the product moment correlation coefficient between p and s.

(c) Explain why your answer to (b) might suggest that there is a linear relationship between p and s.

(d) Find the regression equation of y on x.

(e) Find the regression equation of s on p.

(f) Use the regression equation to predict the bleep score of a person whose pulse rate is 75 beats per minute.

3 The table shows the age (a years) and the mean systolic blood pressure (p mmHg) of a random sample of 10 patients at a doctor's surgery.

When these data are coded by $x = a - 40$ and $y = p - 120$, the following sums are obtained.

$\Sigma x = 99$, $\Sigma y = 191$, $\Sigma x^2 = 2141$, $\Sigma y^2 = 6089$, $\Sigma xy = 3279$

(a) Calculate the p.m.c.c. between x and y.

(b) Does your answer to (a) suggest that there is a linear relationship between a and p? Give reasons for your answer.

(c) Calculate the least squares regression equation of y on x.

(d) Hence find the least squares regression equation of p on a.

(e) (i) Use your regression equation to predict the mean systolic blood pressure of a patient aged 60.

(ii) Comment on how accurate you would expect this prediction to be, giving a reason for your answer.

a	p
63	156
50	131
54	150
49	141
35	109
43	152
53	145
42	126
72	159
38	122

Key points

- Correlation is a measure of how well a bivariate set of data follows a linear relationship. Correlation can be measured by the product moment correlation coefficient, which is given by

$$r = \frac{S_{xy}}{\sqrt{S_{xx}S_{yy}}}$$

where $S_{xy} = \Sigma xy - \dfrac{(\Sigma x)(\Sigma y)}{n}$ $\quad S_{xx} = \Sigma x^2 - \dfrac{(\Sigma x)^2}{n}$ $\quad S_{yy} = \Sigma y^2 - \dfrac{(\Sigma y)^2}{n}$

The p.m.c.c. always lies in the range $-1 \le r \le 1$.
$r = 1$ indicates perfect positive correlation.
$r = -1$ indicates perfect negative correlation.
$r = 0$ indicates no (linear) correlation. (p 72)

- If one or more of the variables is scaled using a linear transformation, then this does not affect the value of r. (p 74)

Test yourself (answers p 135)

1 A company owns two petrol stations P and Q along a main road. Total daily sales in the same week for P ($£p$) and for Q ($£q$) are summarised in the table below.

	p	q
Monday	4760	5380
Tuesday	5395	4460
Wednesday	5840	4640
Thursday	4650	5450
Friday	5365	4340
Saturday	4990	5550
Sunday	4365	5840

When these data are coded using $x = \dfrac{p - 4365}{100}$ and $y = \dfrac{q - 4340}{100}$,

$\Sigma x = 48.1$, $\Sigma y = 52.8$, $\Sigma x^2 = 486.44$, $\Sigma y^2 = 613.22$, $\Sigma xy = 204.95$

(a) Calculate S_{xy}, S_{xx} and S_{yy}.

(b) Calculate, to three significant figures, the value of the product moment correlation coefficient between x and y.

(c) (i) Write down the value of the product moment correlation coefficient between p and q.

   (ii) Give an interpretation of this value.

Edexcel

2 A local authority is investigating the cost of reconditioning its incinerators.
Data from 10 randomly chosen incinerators were collected.
The variables monitored were the operating time x (in thousands of hours) since last reconditioning and the reconditioning cost y (in £1000).
None of the incinerators had been used for more than 3000 hours since last reconditioning.

The data are summarised below.

$\Sigma x = 25.01,\ \Sigma y = 65.68,\ \Sigma x^2 = 50.0,\ \Sigma y^2 = 260.48,\ \Sigma xy = 130.64$

(a) Find S_{xx}, S_{xy}, S_{yy}.

(b) Calculate the product moment correlation coefficient between x and y.

(c) Explain why this value might support the fitting of a linear regression model of the form $y = a + bx$.

(d) Find the values of a and b.

(e) Give an interpretation of a.

(f) Estimate

    (i) the reconditioning cost for an operating time of 2400 hours

    (ii) the financial effect of an increase of 1500 hours in operating time

(g) Suggest why the authority might be cautious about making a prediction of the reconditioning cost of an incinerator which had been operating for 4500 hours since its last reconditioning. Edexcel

3 An agricultural researcher collected data, in appropriate units, on the annual rainfall x and the annual yield of wheat y at 8 randomly selected places.

The data were coded using $s = x - 6$ and $t = y - 20$ and the following summations were obtained.

$\Sigma s = 48.5,\ \Sigma t = 65.0,\ \Sigma s^2 = 402.11,\ \Sigma t^2 = 701.80,\ \Sigma st = 523.23$

(a) Find the equation of the regression line of t on s in the form $t = p + qs$.

(b) Find the equation of the regression line of y on x in the form $y = a + bx$, giving a and b to three decimal places.

The value of the product moment correlation coefficient between s and t is 0.943, to 3 decimal places.

(c) Write down the value of the product moment correlation coefficient between x and y. Give a justification for your answer. Edexcel

6 Discrete random variables

In this chapter you will learn
- what is meant by a discrete random variable, a probability function and a cumulative distribution function
- how to find the mean, variance and standard deviation of a discrete random variable

A Probability functions (answers p 135)

'Senet' is a board game known to have been played in ancient Egypt. Instead of dice, four 'sticks' are thrown. Each stick is rounded on one side and flat on the other. The score depends on the number of sticks that land flat side up.

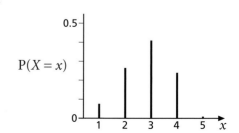

Score 3

Number of flat sides up	0	1	2	3	4
Score	5	1	2	3	4

By throwing the four sticks a large number of times, an experimenter produced the following table of probabilities for the different scores.

Score	1	2	3	4	5
Probability	0.08	0.26	0.41	0.24	0.01

The score is an example of a **discrete random variable**.

 A discrete random variable is a variable that can take individual values (usually integers), each with a given probability.

Let X stand for the score. (Capital letters are used for random variables.) $P(X = 3)$ means the probability that the score is 3. So $P(X = 3) = 0.41$.

The complete set of probabilities for all the possible values of X is called the **probability distribution** of X.

x	1	2	3	4	5
$P(X = x)$	0.08	0.26	0.41	0.24	0.01

Notice that the small letter x is used for individual values of the random variable X.

$P(X = x)$ can be thought of as a function of x. It is called the **probability function** of the discrete random variable X.

A1 What is the sum of all the probabilities in the table?

The probability function can also be shown as a 'stick graph'. The total of the heights of the sticks is 1.

The probability function would be useful to someone wanting to design a computer version of Senet. The scoring device would need to have this distribution if it were to behave like the Senet sticks.

A2 A board game is played with an ordinary dice.
A player moves 1 square if the dice shows one, two or three,
2 squares if it shows four or five and 3 squares if it shows six.

The random variable X is the number of squares moved.
Copy and complete this table of the probability
function of X.

x	1	2	3
$P(X = x)$			

A3 In a game, two ordinary dice are thrown together. The number of squares moved
is 0 if both dice show less than four, 2 if both show more than four, and 1 otherwise.

The random variable Y is the number of squares moved.
Make a table showing the values of $P(Y = y)$ for $y = 0, 1$ and 2.

Discrete uniform distribution

The simplest type of probability distribution
is one where all the probabilities are equal
(as, for example, with the score on a fair dice).
Such a distribution is called **uniform**.

The discrete random variable X shown in this
stick graph has a uniform distribution.

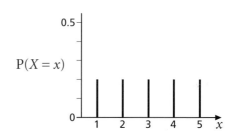

Exercise A (answers p 135)

1 A company that makes games has the idea of using a dice in the shape
of a cuboctahedron. This has two kinds of face, squares and triangles.

The company makes a prototype dice and rolls it 500 times. It lands
with square uppermost 300 times and triangle uppermost 200 times.

(a) Write down the estimates of the probabilities of 'square' and 'triangle'.

In the planned game, two of the dice are rolled.
If both land triangle uppermost the player scores 3.
If both land square uppermost the player scores 2.
Otherwise the player scores 1.

(b) Let X be the score. Using a tree diagram or otherwise, find $P(X = 1)$,
$P(X = 2)$ and $P(X = 3)$.
Make a table and a stick graph showing the probability function of X.

2 A pack contains four cards: Ace, King, Queen, Jack.
In a game played with this pack, the scoring system is as follows.

Pick a card at random: if it is the Ace, score 3; if it isn't, pick again without
replacing the first card. If the card picked this time is the Ace, score 2;
otherwise pick again without replacing. If you get the Ace this time, score 1.
Otherwise score 0.

(a) With the help of a tree diagram, make a table of the probability
function of the score X. Sketch a stick graph of the distribution.

(b) What type of distribution does the discrete random variable X follow?

3 Two children play a game where they roll two ordinary dice.
The score D is the difference between the numbers on the dice.
(The difference is always positive.)

(a) Copy and complete the table on the right which shows the value of D for every possible outcome.

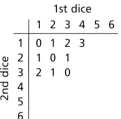

	1st dice					
2nd dice	1	2	3	4	5	6
1	0	1	2	3		
2	1	0	1			
3	2	1	0			
4						
5						
6						

(b) Copy and complete this table to show the probability function of D.

d	0	1	2	3	4	5
$P(D = d)$	$\frac{6}{36}$					

(c) Sketch a stick graph of the distribution.

(d) One child suggests a simple dice game:

'I win if the difference is less than 3; you win if the difference is 3 or more.'

Is this a fair game?
If not, suggest a different but fair rule for winning, still based on differences.

4 A game is played with a single ordinary dice. The scoring system is as follows.

Roll a six first time: score 3; otherwise roll again.
Roll a six second time: score 2; otherwise roll again.
Roll a six third time: score 1; otherwise score 0.

Make a table for the probability function of the score, S.

B Formulae for probability functions (answers p 136)

The probability function of the score X from a single throw of a dice is as follows.

x	1	2	3	4	5	6
$P(X = x)$	$\frac{1}{6}$	$\frac{1}{6}$	$\frac{1}{6}$	$\frac{1}{6}$	$\frac{1}{6}$	$\frac{1}{6}$

This function can be summarised as

$$P(X = x) = \begin{cases} \frac{1}{6} & x = 1, 2, 3, 4, 5, 6 \\ 0 & \text{otherwise} \end{cases}$$

The '0 otherwise' statement shows that the random variable X can only take the values 1, 2, 3, 4, 5, 6.

Other probability functions may be given as formulae in terms of x, for example

$$P(X = x) = \begin{cases} \dfrac{x}{10} & x = 1, 2, 3, 4 \\ 0 & \text{otherwise} \end{cases}$$

In this example, $P(X = 1) = \frac{1}{10}$, $P(X = 2) = \frac{2}{10}$, and so on.

B1 Find the sum of all the probabilities, that is $\sum P(X = x)$, for this distribution.
Why must this always be the value of $\sum P(X = x)$?

B2 A discrete random variable X has the probability function given by

$$P(X = x) = \begin{cases} \dfrac{x+3}{18} & x = 0, 1, 2, 3 \\ 0 & \text{otherwise} \end{cases}$$

Find the values of $P(X = 0)$, $P(X = 1)$, $P(X = 2)$ and $P(X = 3)$, and check that $\sum P(X = x) = 1$.

B3 Explain why the function below cannot be the probability function of a discrete random variable.

$$P(X = x) = \begin{cases} \dfrac{x}{20} & x = 1, 2, 3, 4, 5, 6 \\ 0 & \text{otherwise} \end{cases}$$

B4 It is suggested that the following is the probability function of a discrete random variable X.

$$P(X = x) = \begin{cases} \dfrac{4-x}{5} & x = 1, 2, 3, 4, 5 \\ 0 & \text{otherwise} \end{cases}$$

(a) Find $P(X = x)$ for $x = 1, 2, 3, 4, 5$.

(b) Find $\sum P(X = x)$.

(c) Explain why the function cannot be the probability function of a random variable.

For a function to be the probability function of a discrete random variable, the following must be true.

- The function must give values in the range 0 to 1, otherwise they cannot be probabilities.
- $\sum P(X = x)$ must be equal to 1.

$P(X = x)$ may also be written as $p(x)$.
For example, $p(4)$ would mean the same as $P(X = 4)$, the probability that X takes the value 4.

Modelling a real situation

Discrete random variables are often used to help study a real situation.

For example, suppose a couple would like a child of a particular sex, say male. Their first child may be a boy, or they may have 1, 2, 3, … girls before getting a boy. This situation can be modelled mathematically by making some simplifying assumptions.

We can model the process of having a child by rolling a dice. If the score on the dice is even, this will mean a boy and if odd a girl. Two assumptions are made here:

(1) the outcome of births are independent of each other

(2) a baby is equally likely to be a boy or a girl

Carry out this simple experiment yourself:

Roll a dice and record the roll (1st, 2nd, 3rd, …) on which you first get an even score. Do this about 30 times, making a tally of the number of rolls needed each time.

From your data, estimate the probability of getting an even score for the first time on the 1st, 2nd, 3rd, … roll.

For this model we can calculate the probability of needing 1, 2, 3, … rolls.

The probability of getting an even number on the first roll is $\frac{1}{2}$.

The probability of getting odd, even is $\frac{1}{2} \times \frac{1}{2} = \frac{1}{4}$

The probability of getting odd, odd, even is $\frac{1}{2} \times \frac{1}{2} \times \frac{1}{2} = \frac{1}{8}$, and so on.

So the number of births required for a child of the desired sex to be born can be modelled by the discrete random variable X whose probability function is given by

$$P(X = x) = \frac{1}{2^x} \qquad x = 1, 2, 3, \dots$$

Notice that in this formula there is no limit to the value of x. In reality, of course, there is a limit and this is one way in which the model does not exactly reflect reality. (Another is that the probabilities of a boy and a girl are slightly different.) However, the model might still be a useful tool for studying, for example, what could happen in societies which attach importance to having male heirs.

Example 1

A probability function is given as $\qquad P(X = x) = \begin{cases} kx & x = 1, 2, 3, 4, 5, 6 \\ 0 & \text{otherwise} \end{cases}$

(a) Find the value of k.   (b) Find $P(X \geq 4)$.

Solution

(a) The probability function is shown in this table.

x	1	2	3	4	5	6
$P(X = x)$	k	$2k$	$3k$	$4k$	$5k$	$6k$

$\sum P(X = x)$ must be equal to 1.

So $k + 2k + 3k + 4k + 5k + 6k = 1 \implies 21k = 1 \implies k = \frac{1}{21}$

(b) $P(X \geq 4) = P(X = 4, 5 \text{ or } 6) = P(X = 4) + P(X = 5) + P(X = 6)$

$$= \frac{4}{21} + \frac{5}{21} + \frac{6}{21} = \frac{15}{21} = \frac{5}{7}$$

Exercise B (answers p 136)

1 The probability function of a discrete random variable X is defined by

$$P(X = x) = \begin{cases} \frac{1}{15}x & x = 1, 2, 3, 4, 5 \\ 0 & \text{otherwise} \end{cases}$$

Find $P(X = 1)$, $P(X = 2)$, $P(X = 3)$, $P(X = 4)$ and $P(X = 5)$, and show that they add up to 1.

2 A newsagent notices that no customer buys more than four newspapers or magazines. They are also more likely to buy two or three than one or four.

A student suggests that the number bought might be modelled by a discrete random variable X with the following probability function.

$$p(x) = \begin{cases} \frac{1}{20}x(5 - x) & x = 1, 2, 3, 4 \\ 0 & \text{otherwise} \end{cases}$$

Find $p(1)$, $p(2)$, $p(3)$ and $p(4)$, and draw a stick graph of this probability function.

3 The number of flowers on plants of a certain species is modelled as a discrete random variable X with the probability function $P(X = x)$ as defined below.

$$P(X = x) = \begin{cases} kx^2 & x = 1, 2, 3, 4 \\ 0 & \text{otherwise} \end{cases}$$

(a) Write down, in terms of k, the values of $P(X = 1)$, $P(X = 2)$, $P(X = 3)$ and $P(X = 4)$.

(b) Find the value of k.

(c) Find $P(X \geq 3)$.

4 The probability function of a discrete random variable is given by

$$p(x) = \begin{cases} k(4 - x) & x = 1, 2, 3 \\ k(x - 3) & x = 4 \\ 0 & \text{otherwise} \end{cases}$$

Find the value of k.

C Cumulative distribution function (answers p 136)

A discrete random variable X has the probability function shown here.

x	0	1	2	3	4	5
$P(X = x)$	0.05	0.15	0.30	0.25	0.15	0.10

C1 Find (a) $P(X \leq 3)$ (b) $P(X \leq 6)$ (c) $P(X > 2)$ (d) $P(1 < X \leq 4)$

C2 Find (a) $P(X \leq 3.2)$ (b) $P(X \leq 1.9)$ (c) $P(X > 2.4)$ (d) $P(2.2 \leq X \leq 4.7)$

Calculations involving inequalities are often more easily done from a table of **cumulative** probabilities. This table is made by adding up the probabilities, starting at the left. For example, the cumulative probability corresponding to $x = 3$ is $0.05 + 0.15 + 0.30 + 0.25 = 0.75$. This is $P(X \leq 3)$.

The complete table of cumulative probabilities is as shown here.

x	0	1	2	3	4	5
$P(X \leq x)$	0.05	0.20	0.50	0.75	0.90	1

The function shown in this table is called the **cumulative distribution function**, and is denoted by F.

This function is defined for values between the possible values of X, as well as for the possible values themselves.

For example, $F(2.7) = P(X \leq 2.7)$

$\qquad\qquad = P(X \leq 2)$ (because the only possible values ≤ 2.7 are 0, 1, 2)

$\qquad\qquad = 0.50$

C3 For the random variable X defined above, find

(a) $F(1.6)$ (b) $F(4.1)$ (c) $F(0.3)$ (d) $F(5.5)$ (e) $F(10)$

If a is any given number (not necessarily a possible value of the random variable), then $F(a)$ is the probability that the random variable X is less than or equal to a.

This is the sum of all the individual probabilities $p(x)$ for values of x that are less than or equal to a. So the definition of the cumulative distribution function F can be written as

$$F(a) = P(X \leq a) = \sum_{x \leq a} p(x)$$

Example 2

The probability function of a discrete random variable is given by

$$p(x) = \begin{cases} \dfrac{x}{10} & x = 1, 2, 3, 4 \\ 0 & \text{otherwise} \end{cases}$$

Find $F(3.5)$.

Solution

$$F(3.5) = P(X \leq 3.5) = p(1) + p(2) + p(3) = \tfrac{1}{10} + \tfrac{2}{10} + \tfrac{3}{10} = \tfrac{6}{10}$$

Example 3

The cumulative distribution function of a discrete random variable Y that takes only positive integral values is given in this table.

y	0	1	2	3	4	5
$F(y)$	0.1	0.3	0.6	0.8	0.9	1

Find   **(a)** $F(3)$ **(b)** $F(4.2)$ **(c)** $P(Y = 3)$

Solution

(a) $F(3) = 0.8$ (from table)

(b) Y cannot take values between 4 and 5.
So $F(4.2)$, which is $P(Y \leq 4.2)$, is the same as $F(4)$.
So $F(4.2) = F(4) = 0.9$ (from table)

(c) $P(Y = 3) = P(Y \leq 3) - P(Y \leq 2)$
$\qquad\qquad = F(3) - F(2) = 0.8 - 0.6 = 0.2$

Exercise C (answers p 136)

1 The probability distribution of a discrete random variable X is given in this table.

x	1	2	3	4	5
$P(X = x)$	0.1	0.2	0.4	0.2	0.1

Find   **(a)** $F(3)$ **(b)** $F(4)$ **(c)** $F(3.6)$ **(d)** $F(0.5)$

2 The probability function of a discrete random variable is

$$p(x) = \begin{cases} \frac{1}{40}x(7-x) & x = 1, 2, 3, 4 \\ 0 & \text{otherwise} \end{cases}$$

Make a table of the cumulative distribution function $F(x)$.

3 The cumulative distribution function of a discrete random variable X that can take only positive integer values is shown in this table.

x	1	2	3	4	5
$F(x)$	0.1	0.2	0.4	0.7	1.0

Write out a table showing the probability function $p(x) = P(X = x)$.

4 The probability function of a discrete random variable X is defined as follows.

$$p(x) = \begin{cases} \dfrac{x-1}{25} & x = 2, 3, 4, 5, 6 \\ \dfrac{11-x}{25} & x = 7, 8, 9, 10 \\ 0 & \text{otherwise} \end{cases}$$

(a) Check that $\sum p(x) = 1$.　　　　**(b)** Find the value of $F(6)$

5 The probability function of a discrete random variable X is defined as follows.

$$p(x) = \begin{cases} \dfrac{1}{6} & x = 0 \\ \dfrac{6-x}{k} & x = 1, 2, 3, 4, 5 \\ 0 & \text{otherwise} \end{cases}$$

(a) Find the value of k.　　　　**(b)** Find the value of $F(3)$.

6 The probability function of a discrete random variable is given by

$$p(x) = \begin{cases} k(5-x) & x = 1, 2, 3, 4 \\ k(x-4) & x = 5, 6, 7, 8 \\ 0 & \text{otherwise} \end{cases}$$

(a) Find the value of k.　　　　**(b)** Find the value of $F(7)$.

7 The probability function of a discrete random variable is given by

$$p(x) = \begin{cases} kx^2 & x = 1, 2, 3, 4 \\ k(9-x)^2 & x = 5, 6, 7, 8 \\ 0 & \text{otherwise} \end{cases}$$

(a) Find the value of k.　　　　**(b)** Find the value of $F(6)$.

D Mean, variance and standard deviation (answers p 136)

Here again is the probability function of the
score X when throwing the Senet sticks.

x	1	2	3	4	5
P($X = x$)	0.08	0.26	0.41	0.24	0.01

Imagine throwing the sticks 100 times.
The number of times you would expect to get a score of 1 would be $100 \times 0.08 = 8$.
Similarly, a score of 2 would be expected 26 times, and so on.

These frequencies can be used to calculate a mean score.

$$\text{Mean score} = \frac{(1 \times 8) + (2 \times 26) + (3 \times 41) + (4 \times 24) + (5 \times 1)}{100} = 2.84 \text{ (to 2 d.p.)}$$

It was unnecessary to multiply all the probabilities by 100 and then divide by 100 at the end.
The mean score can be calculated using the probabilities themselves:

$$\text{Mean score} = (1 \times 0.08) + (2 \times 0.26) + (3 \times 0.41) + (4 \times 0.24) + (5 \times 0.01)$$
$$= 2.84 \text{ (to 2 d.p.)}$$

2.84 is the mean of the random variable X.
It is also called the **expected value** of X, and is written E(X).
To calculate it, each possible value of the random variable is multiplied
by its probability, and the products are added together.

$$\text{E}(X) = \sum x \times \text{P}(X = x)$$

D1 Find the mean of the random variable X whose
probability function is shown in this table.

x	0	1	2	3
P($X = x$)	0.35	0.3	0.2	0.15

Imagine a gambling machine on which you pay £1 to play.
Suppose the payout could be zero (with probability 0.7)
or £2 (with probability 0.2) or £5 (with probability 0.1).

The payout in pounds, X, is a discrete random variable
with the probability function shown in this table.

x	0	2	5
P($X = x$)	0.7	0.2	0.1

D2 Find the value of E(X).
What does it tell you about the machine? (Remember you pay £1 to play.)

D3 On another machine you pay 50p per game. The payout is £0 (with probability 0.75)
or £1 (with probability 0.2) or £10 (with probability 0.05).

Let Y be the payout in pounds on one play of this machine.

(a) Make a table of the probability function of Y.

(b) Calculate E(Y).

(c) From the player's point of view, is this machine better or worse than
the previous one?

D4 Gemma suggests a dice game to her brother Carl.
Carl is to roll two ordinary dice.

If the two numbers are equal, Gemma will give him 20p.

If they differ by one, she will give him 5p.

If they differ by more than one, he will give Gemma 10p.

The amount that Carl could win could be −10p (10p loss), 5p or 20p.

(a) Work out the probability of each of the three outcomes (as a fraction).
Let X represent Carl's winnings in a single game.
Make a table of the probability function for X.

x	−10	5	20
P($X = x$)			

(b) Find E(X). What does this tell you about the game?

D5 Gemma suggest a different game. Carl is to roll three ordinary dice.

If the three numbers are all even, Gemma will give him 20p.

If the three numbers are all odd, she will give him 50p.

If the numbers are a mixture of odd and even, Carl will give her 10p.

(a) Let Y represent Carl's winnings in this game.
Make a table of the probability function for Y.

(b) Find E(Y). What does it tell you about the game?

D6 The probability functions for the scores X and Y in two different games are given below.

Game A

x	0	1	2	3	4
P($X = x$)	0.15	0.25	0.25	0.25	0.10

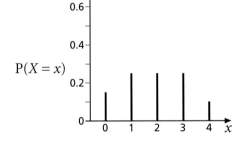

Game B

y	0	1	2	3	4
P($Y = y$)	0.05	0.25	0.50	0.15	0.05

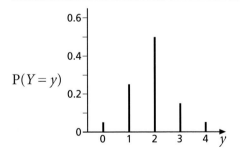

(a) Calculate E(X) and E(Y).

(b) The distributions are alike as far as the mean score is concerned.
What is different about them?

The **variance** of a random variable is defined in a similar way to the variance of a frequency distribution. The score X in game A in question D6 will be used here as an example.

The mean of a random variable is usually denoted by μ.
In this case, $\mu = 1.9$.

The deviation of each possible value from the mean is found. This is $x - \mu$.

Each deviation is squared: $(x - \mu)^2$.

Each squared deviation is multiplied by the corresponding probability $P(X = x)$.

x	$x - \mu$	$(x - \mu)^2$	$P(X = x)$	$(x - \mu)^2 \times P(X = x)$
0	−1.9	3.61	0.15	0.5415
1	−0.9	0.81	0.25	0.2025
2	0.1	0.01	0.25	0.0025
3	1.1	1.21	0.25	0.3025
4	2.1	4.41	0.10	0.4410

Variance = 1.49

The total, 1.49, is the variance of X, denoted by Var(X).

D7 When calculating the variance of a frequency distribution, you divide the total of all the squared deviations by the total frequency. Why is it unnecessary in the case of a random variable to divide by the total probability?

The **standard deviation** of a random variable is denoted by σ.
This is the square root of the variance, so the variance is σ^2.

In the example above, $\sigma^2 = 1.49$, so $\sigma = \sqrt{1.49} = 1.22$ (to 3 s.f.).

The definitions of the mean and variance are

K

$E(X) = \mu = \sum x_i \times P(X = x_i)$ or $\sum x_i p_i$

$Var(X) = \sigma^2 = \sum (x_i - \mu)^2 \times P(X = x_i)$ or $\sum (x_i - \mu)^2 p_i$

where p_i are the corresponding probabilities of the values x_i.

As in the case of a frequency distribution, an equivalent expression for the variance is easier to use in practice. (It is proved on page 100.)

$\sigma^2 = \sum x_i^2 \times P(X = x_i) - \mu^2$ or $\sum x_i^2 p_i - \mu^2$

D8 Calculate the variance and standard deviation of the score in game B in question D6.
Which of the two games has the wider variation in scores?
How could you also tell this from the graphs?

Example 4

The probability function of a discrete random variable X is given in this table.

Find $E(X)$ and Var(X).

x	1	2	3	4
$P(X = x)$	0.1	0.2	0.3	0.4

Solution

$E(X) = (1 \times 0.1) + (2 \times 0.2) + (3 \times 0.3) + (4 \times 0.4) = 3$

$Var(X) = \sum x_i^2 p_i - \mu^2$

$= [(1^2 \times 0.1) + (2^2 \times 0.2) + (3^2 \times 0.3) + (4^2 \times 0.4)] - 3^2 = 10 - 9 = 1$

Example 5

The probability function of the discrete random variable X is shown in the table.
Given that $E(X) = 2.95$, find the values of a and b.

x	1	2	3	4
$P(X = x)$	0.2	a	0.25	b

Solution

The total probability must be 1, so $a + b = 0.55$ (1)

$E(X) = 2.95$, so $(1 \times 0.2) + 2a + (3 \times 0.25) + 4b = 2.95$

$\Rightarrow \quad 2a + 4b = 2$ or $a + 2b = 1$ (2)

By subtracting (1) from (2), $b = 1 - 0.55 = 0.45$, from which $a = 0.55 - 0.45 = 0.1$

Exercise D (answers p 137)

1 The probability function of the score S on an ordinary dice is shown here.
Calculate

s	1	2	3	4	5	6
$P(S = s)$	$\frac{1}{6}$	$\frac{1}{6}$	$\frac{1}{6}$	$\frac{1}{6}$	$\frac{1}{6}$	$\frac{1}{6}$

(a) the mean of S (b) the variance of S (c) the standard deviation of S

2 Two ordinary dice are rolled. The score D is the difference between the two numbers (as in exercise A, question 3).
Here is the probability function of D.
Calculate

d	0	1	2	3	4	5
$P(D = d)$	$\frac{6}{36}$	$\frac{10}{36}$	$\frac{8}{36}$	$\frac{6}{36}$	$\frac{4}{36}$	$\frac{2}{36}$

(a) the mean of D (b) the variance of D (c) the standard deviation of D

3 The diagram shows a fair spinner.
Let X be the score when the spinner is spun.
The table shows part of the probability function of X.

x	1	2	3
$P(X = x)$	$\frac{1}{2}$		

(a) Copy and complete the table.

(b) Calculate the mean of X.

(c) Calculate the variance of X.

4 The probability function of a discrete random variable X is defined by

$$p(x) = \begin{cases} \frac{1}{15}x & x = 1, 2, 3, 4, 5 \\ 0 & \text{otherwise} \end{cases}$$

Find $E(X)$ and $Var(X)$.

5 The probability function of a discrete random variable X is given by

$$p(x) = \begin{cases} k(20 - x^2) & x = 1, 2, 3, 4 \\ 0 & \text{otherwise} \end{cases}$$

(a) Find the value of k. (b) Find $E(X)$. (c) Find $Var(X)$.

6 A uniform distribution is defined by the following probability function.

$$p(x) = \begin{cases} \frac{1}{5} & x = 1, 2, 3, 4, 5 \\ 0 & \text{otherwise} \end{cases}$$

(a) Find $E(X)$ and $Var(X)$.

(b) Y is a uniformly distributed random variable that can take the values 1, 2, 3, 4, ..., 10. Find $E(Y)$.

(c) What is the mean of a uniform distribution with values 1, 2, 3, 4, ..., n?

7 The probability function of a discrete random variable Y is shown in the table.

y	0	1	2	3
$P(Y = y)$	α	0.3	0.4	β

(a) Given that $E(Y) = 1.4$, find the value of β. Hence find the value of α.

(b) Find $Var(Y)$.

8 The probability distribution of a discrete random variable X is given by this table.

x	0	1	2	3
$P(X = x)$	α	0.3	0.3	β

Given that $E(X) = 1.8$,

(a) find α and β (b) find $Var(X)$

E Functions of a discrete random variable (answers p 137)

Suppose a tetrahedral dice has the numbers 1, 2, 3, 4 on its faces. The score X from a single throw of this dice has the probability function shown in this table.

Value of X	1	2	3	4
Probability	$\frac{1}{4}$	$\frac{1}{4}$	$\frac{1}{4}$	$\frac{1}{4}$

In a game, this dice is thrown and the score doubled. The 'double score' is a random variable. Call it Y. Then $Y = 2X$ and the probability function of Y is as shown. Each value of X is doubled; the probabilities stay the same.

Value of Y	2	4	6	8
Probability	$\frac{1}{4}$	$\frac{1}{4}$	$\frac{1}{4}$	$\frac{1}{4}$

E1 (a) Find the expected value and the variance of X.

(b) Do the same for Y, where $Y = 2X$.

(c) What is the relationship between

(i) $E(Y)$ and $E(X)$ (ii) $Var(Y)$ and $Var(X)$

E2 In a different game with the same dice, 3 is added to the score. This gives the random variable W, where $W = X + 3$.

(a) Make a table for the probability function of W.

(b) Find $E(W)$ and $Var(W)$.

(c) How are the expected values of W and X related?

(d) How are the variances of W and X related?

E3 Suppose the dice score is doubled and then 3 is added. This gives the random variable V, where $V = 2X + 3$.

Value of V	5			
Probability	$\frac{1}{4}$	$\frac{1}{4}$	$\frac{1}{4}$	$\frac{1}{4}$

(a) Copy and complete this table for the probability function of V.

(b) Find $E(V)$ and $Var(V)$.

(c) What is the relationship between

    (i) $E(V)$ and $E(X)$ (ii) $Var(V)$ and $Var(X)$

K In general, if $Y = aX + b$, then the mean and variance of Y are related to those of X by the equations

$$E(Y) = aE(X) + b \qquad Var(Y) = a^2 Var(X)$$

The reasons are as follows.

(1) First suppose that each possible value $x_1, x_2, x_3, \ldots$ is multiplied by a.

To find the new mean we have to calculate $ax_1 p_1 + ax_2 p_2 + ax_3 p_3 + \ldots$
$$= a(x_1 p_1 + x_2 p_2 + x_3 p_3 + \ldots)$$

So multiplying every value by a results in the mean being multiplied by a.

(2) Now suppose that every possible value is increased by b.

The new mean is $(x_1 + b)p_1 + (x_2 + b)p_2 + (x_3 + b)p_3 + \ldots$
$$= (x_1 p_1 + x_2 p_2 + x_3 p_3 + \ldots) + b(p_1 + p_2 + p_3 + \ldots)$$

Because $p_1 + p_2 + p_3 + \ldots = 1$, it follows that adding b to each value results in adding b to the mean.

(3) If we both multiply each value by a and then add b, the mean is first multiplied by a and then b is added. So $E(aX + b) = aE(X) + b$.

(4) The variance involves the squared deviations from the mean.

If b is added to every value, it gets added to the mean as well, from (2).

So the deviations from the mean are not changed and so there is no effect on the variance.

(5) If every value is multiplied by a, so is the mean. So every deviation from the mean is also multiplied by a. When the deviations are squared, they are each multiplied by a^2. So the variance is multiplied by a^2.

(6) If we both multiply each value by a and then add b, the variance is multiplied by a^2 but adding the b to each value has no effect. So $Var(aX + b) = a^2 Var(X)$.

One other function is important in applications, the function X^2.

If the possible values of a random variable X are $x_1, x_2, x_3, \ldots$, then the corresponding values of X^2 are $x_1^2, x_2^2, x_3^2, \ldots$

So $E(X^2) = x_1^2 p_1 + x_2^2 p_2 + x_3^2 p_3 + \ldots$

But this is the expression that appears in the calculating formula $\sigma^2 = \Sigma x_i^2 p_i - \mu^2$.

K So the formula can be written

$$Var(X) = \sigma^2 = E(X^2) - [E(X)]^2$$

Example 6

The mean of the score of a single throw of a normal dice is 3.5 with variance $\frac{35}{12}$.
In a game, the score is doubled and 3 subtracted.
What are the mean and variance of the score in this game?

Solution

$E(X) = 3.5$ and $Var(X) = \frac{35}{12}$

so $E(2X - 3) = 2 \times 3.5 - 3 = 4$ and $Var(2X - 3) = 2^2 \times \frac{35}{12} = \frac{35}{3}$

Example 7

The probability function of the discrete random
variable X is shown in the table. Find

x	1	2	3	4
$P(X = x)$	0.1	0.3	0.4	0.2

(a) $E(X)$ (b) $E(X^2)$ (c) $Var(X)$

Solution

(a) $E(X) = (1 \times 0.1) + (2 \times 0.3) + (3 \times 0.4) + (4 \times 0.2) = 2.7$

(b) $E(X^2) = (1^2 \times 0.1) + (2^2 \times 0.3) + (3^2 \times 0.4) + (4^2 \times 0.2) = 8.1$

(c) $Var(X) = E(X^2) - [E(X)]^2 = 8.1 - 2.7^2 = 0.81$

Exercise E (answers p 137)

1 The probability distribution of the score X on a tetrahedral dice is such that
$E(X) = 2.5$ and $Var(X) = 1.25$. Find

(a) $E(3X)$ (b) $E(2X + 3)$ (c) $Var(2X)$ (d) $Var(3X + 2)$

2 X is a discrete random variable for which $E(X) = 4.5$ and $Var(X) = 2.5$.
Find the value of

(a) $E(3X)$ (b) $Var(3X)$ (c) $E(3X + 4)$ (d) $Var(3X + 4)$

(e) $E(-2X)$ (f) $Var(-2X)$ (g) $E(-2X + 7)$ (h) $Var(-2X + 7)$

3 The discrete random variable X has the
probability function given in this table.

x	1	2	3	4
$P(X = x)$	0.2	0.4	0.3	0.1

(a) Find $E(X)$ and $Var(X)$.

(b) Find   (i) $E(3X + 2)$ (ii) $E(4X - 1)$ (iii) $Var(2X - 4)$

4 The probability distribution function of a discrete random variable X is given by

$$p(x) = \begin{cases} k(x^2 - 3) & x = 2, 3, 4 \\ 0 & \text{otherwise} \end{cases}$$

(a) Find the value of k.

(b) Find $E(X)$ and $Var(X)$.

(c) Find   (i) $E(2X + 1)$ (ii) $E\left(\frac{1}{2}X + 2\right)$ (iii) $Var(2X - 7)$

5 The probability function of a discrete random variable X is shown in the table. Find

x	0	1	2	3	4
$P(X = x)$	0.05	0.2	0.35	0.25	0.15

(a) $E(X)$ (b) $E(X^2)$ (c) $Var(X)$ (d) $Var(2X - 1)$

6 A discrete random variable X is such that $E(X) = 8$ and $Var(X) = 3$.
Another discrete random variable Y is defined by $Y = aX + b$.
Given that $E(Y) = 30$ and $Var(Y) = 27$, find the values of a and b.

Key points

- A discrete random variable takes individual values (usually integers), each with a given probability.   (p 82)

- A uniformly distributed discrete random variable has equal probabilities for each of the values it can take.   (p 83)

- The probability function p(x) of a discrete random variable X is the function that gives the probability for each possible value of X, so p$(x) = P(X = x)$.

  The following must be true of a probability function.
  (a) $0 \leq \text{p}(x) \leq 1$ for all values of x
  (b) $\sum \text{p}(x) = 1$ (p 85)

- The cumulative distribution function F is defined by
$$F(a) = P(X \leq a) = \sum_{x \leq a} \text{p}(x)$$
  (p 88)

- The mean of a discrete random variable X is denoted by $E(X)$ or μ. It is defined as $\sum x \times P(X = x)$ or $\sum x_i p_i$, where p_i is the probability of the value x_i.   (pp 90, 92)

- The variance σ^2 is defined by $\sigma^2 = Var(X) = \sum (x_i - \mu)^2 p_i$.
  An equivalent form of this equation is $\sigma^2 = \sum x_i^2 p_i - \mu^2$.
  This can also be written as $Var(X) = E(X^2) - [E(X)]^2$.   (pp 92, 95)

- $E(aX + b) = aE(X) + b$
  $Var(aX + b) = a^2 Var(X)$ (p 95)

Mixed questions (answers p 137)

1 The probability function of a discrete random variable X is shown in the table. Find

x	1	2	3	4	5
$P(X = x)$	0.1	0.2	0.3	0.3	0.1

(a) $E(X)$ (b) $Var(X)$ (c) $F(4.8)$ (d) $E(3X + 2)$ (e) $Var(2X - 6)$

2 The probability function of a discrete random variable is given by

$$p(x) = \begin{cases} kx(8-x) & x = 4, 5, 6, 7 \\ 0 & \text{otherwise} \end{cases}$$

where k is a positive constant.

(a) Find the value of k.   (b) Calculate E(X).   (c) Calculate Var(X).

(d) Find F(6).   (e) Find E$(3X - 2)$.

3 A dice is weighted so that the probability of getting a six is 0.55, and the other numbers are equally likely.

(a) Make a table for the probability function of the score on a single throw of this dice.

(b) Calculate the mean and variance of the score.

4 The discrete random variable X can take only positive integer values. Its cumulative distribution function is shown in this table.

x	1	2	3	4	5
F(x)	0.2	0.5	0.8	0.9	1

Find   (a) P$(X = 3)$ (b) E(X) (c) Var(X)

5 The discrete random variable X has the probability distribution shown in the table.

x	−1	0	1	2	3
P$(X = x)$	α	0.1	0.2	β	0.2

Given that E$(X) = 1.65$, find the values of

(a) α and β (b) E(X^2) (c) Var(X) (d) E$(2X - 1)$ (e) Var$(2X + 3)$

6 The discrete random variable X has the probability distribution shown in the table.

x	−2	−1	0	1	2
P$(X = x)$	α	0.3	β	0.1	0.2

Given that E$(X) = -0.1$, find the values of

(a) α and β (b) E(X^2) (c) Var(X) (d) E$(5 - X)$ (e) Var$(5 - X)$

7 A gambling machine is being designed. The payouts are to be £0, £2, £5 and £20.

The probability of paying out £2 has been fixed at 0.1 and the probability of paying out £5 has been fixed at 0.05.

The other probabilities have not yet been fixed: the probability of paying out £0 is a and the probability of paying out £20 is b.

X represents the payout per game.
The probability function of X is shown in the table.

x	0	2	5	20
P$(X = x)$	a	0.1	0.05	b

(a) Find an expression for E(X).

(b) The machine is fair to the player if the expected value of the payout is equal to the cost of a game. If the cost of a game is £1, what must the values of a and b be for the machine to be fair?

(c) It is decided to fix b at 0.01. The cost of a game is £1.
What is the expected loss per game to the player?

8 A café owner installs two machines, A and B.
On each machine a game costs £2.

For machine A, the payout X, in pounds, has the probability function shown in this table.

x	0	2	5	10	20
$P(X = x)$	0.70	0.10	0.10	0.09	0.01

For machine B, the payout Y, in pounds, has the probability function shown in this table.

y	0	2	5	10	20
$P(Y = y)$	0.82	0.05	0.05	0.02	0.06

(a) Find

    (i) $E(X)$ **(ii)** $Var(X)$ **(iii)** $E(Y)$ **(iv)** $Var(Y)$

(b) Which machine is better from the player's point of view?
Give the reason for your answer.

(c) How much does a player expect to lose, per game, on each machine?

(d) How can you tell by looking at the probability functions that the variance of Y is greater than the variance of X?

Test yourself (answers p 138)

1 The discrete random variable X has the probability function shown in the table below.

x	−2	−1	0	1	2	3
$P(X = x)$	0.1	0.2	0.1	0.3	α	0.1

Find

(a) α (b) $P(-1 < X \le 1)$ (c) $F(-0.2)$

(d) $E(2X - 1)$ (e) $Var(2X + 1)$

2 A fair six-sided dice is rolled. The random variable X represents the score.

(a) Write down the probability function of X.

(b) What type of distribution does X have?

Find the value of

(c) $E(4X + 2)$

(d) $Var(4X - 2)$

3 The discrete random variable X has probability function

$$P(X = x) = \begin{cases} k(x^2 - 9) & x = 4, 5, 6 \\ 0 & \text{otherwise} \end{cases}$$

where k is a positive constant.

(a) Show that $k = \frac{1}{50}$.

(b) Find $E(X)$ and $\text{Var}(X)$.

(c) Find $\text{Var}(2X - 3)$.   Edexcel

4 A discrete random variable X has the probability function shown in the table below.

x	0	1	2
$P(X = x)$	$\frac{1}{3}$	a	$\frac{2}{3} - a$

(a) Given that $E(X) = \frac{5}{6}$, find a.

(b) Find the exact value of $\text{Var}(X)$.

(c) Find the exact value of $P(X \leq 1.5)$.   Edexcel

5 A discrete random variable X takes only positive integer values.
It has a cumulative distribution function $F(x) = P(X \leq x)$ defined in the table below.

x	1	2	3	4	5	6	7	8
$F(x)$	0.1	0.2	0.25	0.4	0.5	0.6	0.75	1.0

(a) Determine the probability function, $P(X = x)$, of X.

(b) Calculate $E(X)$ and show that $\text{Var}(X) = 5.76$.

(c) Given that $Y = 2X + 3$, find the mean and variance of Y.   Edexcel

---

Proof of the calculating formula $\text{Var}(X) = \sum x_i^2 p_i - \mu^2$

$$\begin{aligned}
\text{Var}(X) &= \sum(x_i - \mu)^2 p_i \\
&= \sum(x_i^2 - 2\mu x_i + \mu^2)p_i && \textit{by expanding the brackets} \\
&= \sum x_i^2 p_i - 2\mu \sum x_i p_i + \mu^2 \sum p_i && \textit{by writing the single sum as three separate sums} \\
&= \sum x_i^2 p_i - 2\mu^2 + \mu^2 && \textit{because } \sum x_i p_i = \mu \text{ and } \sum p_i = 1 \\
&= \sum x_i^2 p_i - \mu^2
\end{aligned}$$

7 Normal distribution

In this chapter you will learn
- about the properties of a normal distribution
- how to solve problems using tables of the normal distribution function

A Proportions (answers p 138)

The set of data below shows the weights in grams of 100 2p coins.
The stem-and-leaf diagram displays the values of the second decimal place in two rows
to show the distribution more clearly.

6.8	0
	6
6.9	2 4
	5 6 7 8 8 9
7.0	0 0 0 1 1 1 3 4 4 4
	5 5 5 5 5 6 6 7 7 7 8 8 8 8 9 9 9 9 9
7.1	0 0 0 0 1 1 1 1 1 1 1 1 2 2 2 2 2 3 3 3 4 4 4
	5 5 5 6 6 6 7 7 7 7 7 8 8 8 8 8 9 9 9 9
7.2	0 0 1 2 2 2 3 4 4
	5 6 6 7 9 9
7.3	1 4
7.4	0

> **Key**
> **7.3 | 4**   stands for 7.34

(Mean = 7.117 g; standard deviation = 0.099 g)

The mean weight is 7.117 g and the standard deviation is 0.099 g.

In the work that follows we investigate the proportions of the distribution
that lie in the intervals shown below.

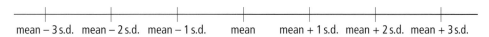

A1 For the data above, one standard deviation above the mean is $7.117 + 0.099 = 7.216$.
Find the values of (mean − 1 s.d.) and the other quantities shown above.

A2 (a) Verify that 34% of the distribution is between the mean and (mean + 1 s.d.).

(b) Find the percentage of the data lying in each of the other intervals.
Use your results to complete the following diagram. (Leave the labels on the
scale as they are: do not replace them with values.)

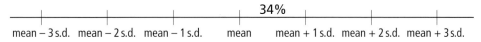

A3 This set of data shows the IQ scores of 120 students at a school.

```
 6 | 3
   |
 7 | 1 2
   | 5
 8 | 1 2 4 4
   | 5 6 6 8 8
 9 | 0 0 0 1 1 1 2 3 4 4 4
   | 5 5 5 6 6 6 7 8 8 8 9 9
10 | 0 0 0 1 1 2 2 2 3 4 4 4 4 4
   | 5 5 5 5 6 6 7 7 7 7 8 8 8 9 9 9
11 | 0 0 0 1 1 1 2 2 2 3 4 4 4 4
   | 5 5 6 6 7 7 7 8 8 8 9 9 9
12 | 0 0 0 1 1 2 3 3 4 4
   | 5 5 5 6 8 8 9 9 9
13 | 0 1 1 1 3
   | 5 7
14 | 3
```

14 | 3   means an IQ of 143

(Mean = 107.4; standard deviation = 15.2)

Complete a diagram for this data like the one in A2.

A4 This data shows the time in minutes that 80 cars stayed in a bay with a one-hour parking limit during one day.

```
0 | 2 2 3 3 4 4 6 6 7 7 8
1 | 0 0 0 0 1 1 1 2 2 3 4 4 5 6 7
2 | 0 3 3 4 4 4 5 5 5 5 8 8 8
3 | 0 0 0 0 2 2 2 4 4 5 6 7 9
4 | 0 2 4 4 5 5 6 6 6 7 8 8 9 9
5 | 1 2 2 2 3 3 4 6 6 6 7 7 8 9
```

5 | 1   means 51 minutes

(Mean = 30.0; standard deviation = 17.5)

Complete a diagram as before for this data.

A5 Comment on any similarities and differences between the three diagrams you have drawn.

The first two sets of data have similar distributions, with similar proportions lying between a given number of standard deviations from the mean. The distribution of the the third set of data is of a different shape and the proportions are different.

Each of the first two distributions is roughly symmetrical about its mean. There is a large proportion of the population around the mean and less towards the 'tails' of the distribution. Such a distribution is often called 'bell-shaped'. The proportion within a given number of standard deviations of the mean is approximately as shown here.

If a population is known to have this bell-shaped distribution, the proportions above can be used to solve simple problems.

A6 The heights of students in a college follow the distribution shown above with mean 165 cm and standard deviation 8 cm.

(a) Explain why the percentage of students shorter than 157 cm is 16%.

(b) Above roughly what height are the tallest 2% of students?

Exercise A (answers p 138)

1 Marks in an examination have the distribution above with mean 45 and standard deviation 12.

(a) Roughly what percentage of marks were less than 33?

(b) Grade C was awarded for a mark within one s.d. above or below the mean. Roughly what percentage of candidates were awarded grade C?

(c) Grade A was awarded for a mark greater than 69.
80 candidates sat the exam.
Estimate how many were awarded grade A.

(d) Anyone who was in the lowest 2% of candidates failed.
Below what mark, roughly, would a candidate fail?

2 IQ tests are designed so that nationally the population has a mean IQ of 100 with standard deviation 15. IQ scores have the distribution above.

(a) Roughly what percentage of people have an IQ less than 70?

(b) Roughly what percentage of people have an IQ between 100 and 115?

(c) An Egghead Society is to be set up which is to include people who have the top 2% of IQs in the country. Roughly what IQ must someone have to join the Egghead Society?

B The standard normal probability distribution

This histogram shows the heights of a very large population (10 000) of men.

As in all histograms frequency is represented by the area of a bar. The frequencies are stated on the graph.

The number of men with heights in the interval from 170 to 180 cm is represented by the shaded area.

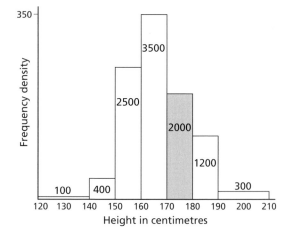

Dividing each of the frequencies by 10 000 gives the proportions that lie in each group.

The areas of the bars now show these proportions. The total area of all the bars is now 1.

The shaded area shows the proportion of men with heights between 170 and 180 cm.

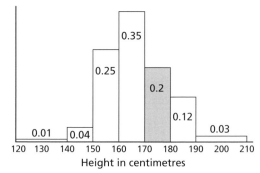

Since the population is large, the groups could be much smaller, say 2 cm wide.

The graph of proportions might then look like this.

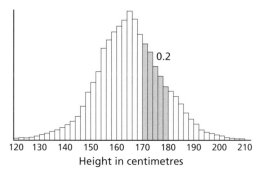

With a large population and small intervals the histogram can be approximated by a curve.
The area under the curve between 170 and 180 cm still represents the proportion of men in this group.

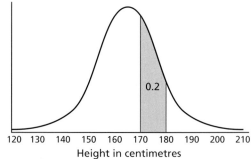

If a man is selected at random from the population, the probability that his height is between 170 cm and 180 cm is 0.2.

Areas under the graph can be interpreted either as proportions or as probabilities.

The height H cm of a randomly selected man is a **continuous random variable**. (As always, random variables are denoted by capital letters.)

The graph shows the **probability distribution** of H.

The probability that H lies between 170 and 180 is written P$(170 < H < 180)$. So P$(170 < H < 180) = 0.2$.

It does not matter whether you use $<$ or $\leq$ in these inequalities, because the probability that H has a particular individual value (say exactly 151.28) is zero. An exact value can be thought of as an interval of zero width, with zero area under the graph.

The distribution of H is bell-shaped. This type of distribution occurs so frequently that mathematicians have looked for a mathematical model to fit the shape.

The equation $f(x) = \dfrac{1}{\sqrt{2\pi}} e^{-\frac{1}{2}x^2}$ has been found to be a very good model.

(e is an irrational number approximately equal to 2.718…)

The graph, obtained from a graph plotter, is shown here.

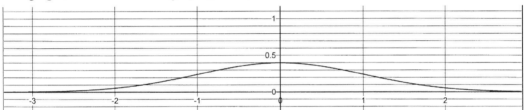

The total area under this curve is 1.
The distribution has a mean of 0 and a standard deviation of 1.

The area under the curve between 0 and 1 gives the probability that a value lies between the mean and one standard deviation above the mean. This probability is 0.3413.

The equation for this distribution was first given by the French mathematician Abraham de Moivre (1667–1754). The distribution is sometimes called the Gaussian distribution after the mathematician Carl Gauss (1777–1855).

The distribution is more commonly known as the **standard normal distribution**.

Finding areas under the standard normal curve from the equation is difficult. However, because many real-life data sets can be related to the standard normal distribution, areas under the curve are often needed in statistics.

A table of these areas is printed in a booklet for use in AS/A2 exams and is reproduced on page 120 of this book.

Using the standard normal distribution table

The function $\Phi(z)$ represents the area under the curve to the left of the value z.

(The Greek capital letter Φ is pronounced 'phi'.)

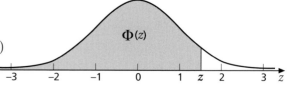

K The letter Z is used to denote a continuous random variable that follows the standard normal distribution.

$\Phi(z)$ is the probability that Z is less than z.

In symbols $\Phi(z) = P(Z < z)$.

Here is part of the standard normal distribution table.

z	$\Phi(z)$	z	$\Phi(z)$	z	$\Phi(z)$
0.00	0.5000	0.50	0.6915	1.00	0.8413
0.01	0.5040	0.51	0.6950	1.01	0.8438
0.02	0.5080	0.52	0.6985	1.02	0.8461
0.03	0.5120	0.53	0.7019	1.03	0.8485
0.04	0.5160	0.54	0.7054	1.04	0.8508
0.05	0.5199	0.55	0.7088	1.05	0.8531
0.06	0.5239	0.56	0.7123	1.06	0.8554

Values of $\Phi(z)$ are not given for negative values of z, because they can be found by subtraction using the symmetry of the curve.

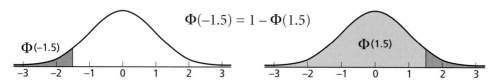

$$\Phi(-1.5) = 1 - \Phi(1.5)$$

Example 1

Use the table to find the area shaded under this standard normal curve.

Solution

From the table, $\Phi(0.8) = 0.7881$

Area $= 1 - 0.7881 = 0.2119$

Example 2

Use the table to find the area shaded here.

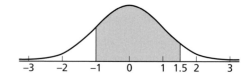

Solution

From the table, $\Phi(1.50) = 0.9332$

$\Phi(-1.00) = 1 - \Phi(1.00) = 1 - 0.8413 = 0.1587$

Shaded area $= \Phi(1.50) - \Phi(-1.00) = 0.9332 - 0.1587 = 0.7745$

Exercise B (answers p 138)

1 Use the table to find the areas shaded under these standard normal curves.

(a)

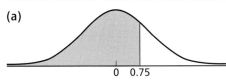

0   0.75

(b)

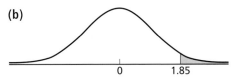

0   1.85

(c)

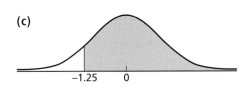

−1.25   0

(d)

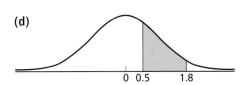

0 0.5   1.8

2 Draw sketches showing the probability that Z lies in each of these ranges.
Use the table to find each probability.

(a) $0 < Z < 1.8$ (b) $1.25 < Z < 3.5$ (c) $-1.5 < Z < 0.85$ (d) $-2.43 < Z < -1.06$

3 Find

(a) $P(Z \geq 1.4)$ (b) $P(Z < -0.7)$ (c) $P(-1.8 \leq Z \leq 0.9)$

(d) $P(0.5 < Z < 2.5)$ (e) $P(-0.4 \leq Z \leq 1.4)$ (f) $P(-1.9 < Z < -0.5)$

4 Use the table to find, to two decimal places, the value of z for which

(a) $\Phi(z) = 0.95$ (b) $\Phi(z) = 0.9$ (c) $\Phi(z) = 0.99$ (d) $\Phi(z) = 0.75$

5 Use the table to find, as accurately as you can, the value of z in these diagrams.

(a)

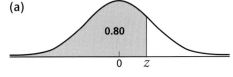

0.80

0   z

(b)

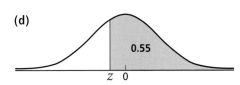

0.15

0   z

(c)

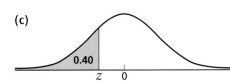

0.40

z   0

(d)

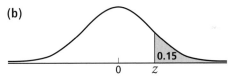

0.55

z 0

6 Find, as accurately as you can, the value of k in each of these diagrams.

(a)

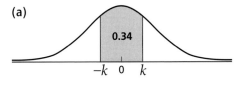

0.34

−k 0   k

(b)

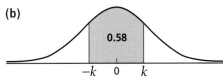

0.58

−k 0   k

C Finding probabilities and proportions

Once we know, or can assume, that a normal distribution is an appropriate model for a population or a random variable, and we know the mean and standard deviation, the proportion or probability for any given interval can be found.

For example, coin-operated machines rely on coins being a certain weight. The weights of 2p coins are known to be normally distributed with mean 7 g and standard deviation 0.1 g.

If W is the weight of a 2p coin, the distribution of W can be related to the standard normal distribution as shown in this diagram.

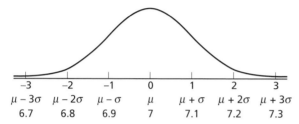

The top row of labels shows values of a standard normal variable.
The second row shows how these relate to a distribution with mean μ and s.d. σ.
The third row shows values for W, for which $\mu = 7$ and $\sigma = 0.1$.

A particular machine rejects coins if they weigh less than 6.85 g.
If we want to know the probability that a randomly selected coin will be rejected, we need to find P($W < 6.85$).

To relate the value 6.85 to the standard normal distribution, we need to know how many standard deviations below the mean this is.

This is found by calculating $\dfrac{6.85 - 7}{0.1} = -1.5$, so 6.85 is 1.5 s.d.s below the mean.

The diagram above confirms this.

> To convert a value of W to a standard normal value, we subtract the mean μ and divide by the standard deviation σ.
>
> The **standard normal variable** Z corresponding to W is given by $Z = \dfrac{W - \mu}{\sigma}$.

Finding P($W < 6.85$) is the same as finding P($Z < -1.5$).

From the standard normal table, $\Phi(1.5) = 0.9332$

So P($Z < -1.5$) = $\Phi(-1.5)$
$= 1 - \Phi(1.5)$
$= 1 - 0.9332 = 0.0668$

That is, roughly 7% of 2p coins will be rejected.

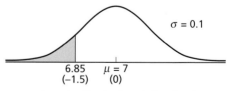

K A normal distribution is completely specified when two **parameters**, the mean (μ) and the standard deviation (σ), are known.

If a variable X has a distribution which is modelled by a normal probability distribution, and has mean μ and standard deviation σ, then this is denoted by

$$X \sim N(\mu, \sigma^2)$$

(Note that the variance is given, not the standard deviation.)

The distribution of the weights in grams of the 2p coins can be denoted by $W \sim N(7, 0.01)$.

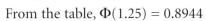

Example 3

The quantity of cola put into a bottle by a filling machine is normally distributed with mean 300 ml and standard deviation 4 ml. A company employee suggests rejecting bottles that contain less than 295 ml. If the suggestion is accepted, what proportion of bottles would be rejected?

Solution

If Q is the quantity put into a bottle, then $Q \sim N(300, 4^2)$.

We require $P(Q < 295)$.

The standardised value for 295 is

$$\frac{295 - 300}{4} = -1.25 \text{ s.d.s from the mean.}$$

From the table, $\Phi(1.25) = 0.8944$

The probability needed here is shown by the shaded area.

$P(Q < 295) = P(Z < -1.25) = 1 - 0.8944 = 0.1056$

So 10.6% of bottles would be rejected.

Example 4

The continuous random variable X is normally distributed with mean 20 and standard deviation 5. Find $P(14 \leq X \leq 28)$.

Solution

The standardised values corresponding to 14 and 28 are $\dfrac{14 - 20}{5} = -1.2$ and $\dfrac{28 - 20}{5} = 1.6$.

So the required probability is $P(-1.2 \leq Z \leq 1.6)$, shown shaded in the diagram.

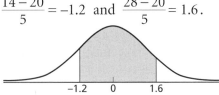

From the table, $\Phi(1.2) = 0.8849$

So $\Phi(-1.2) = 1 - 0.8849 = 0.1151$

From the table, $\Phi(1.6) = 0.9452$

The required probability is $\Phi(1.6) - \Phi(-1.2)$
$$= 0.9452 - 0.1151 = 0.8301$$

Exercise C (answers p 139)

In each of the following questions, assume that the variable is normally distributed.

1 The lifetime of a type of battery has a mean of 10 hours with standard deviation 2 hours. What proportion of batteries have a lifetime

(a) greater than 15 hours   (b) between 8 and 12 hours

2 A machine turns out bolts of mean diameter 1.5 cm and standard deviation 0.01 cm. If bolts measuring over 1.52 cm are rejected as oversize, what proportion are rejected in this way?

3 IQ tests for young people are designed so that nationally they have a mean of 100 and a standard deviation of 15.
What percentage of children have an IQ of 132 or more?

4 The continuous random variable X is normally distributed with mean 50 and standard deviation 10. Find the value of

(a) $P(X > 55)$ (b) $P(X < 35)$ (c) $P(30 \leq X \leq 40)$

5 A machine produces bags of sugar which have mean weight 1.5 kg and standard deviation 0.01 kg. What is the probability of producing a bag of sugar which weighs less than 1.475 kg?

6 Simply More Pure margarine is sold in tubs with a mean weight of 500 g and standard deviation 4 g.
What proportion of tubs weigh between 498.5 g and 500.5 g?

7 The heights of girls in a particular year group have mean 154.2 cm and standard deviation 5.1 cm.
What percentage of the girls are between 150 cm and 155 cm tall?

8 The weight of sweets produced by a machine is modelled by a normal distribution with mean 45 g and standard deviation 5 g.

The random variable W is the weight in grams of a sweet selected at random from the output of the machine. Find

(a) $P(W < 42)$ (b) $P(43 \leq W \leq 47)$

9 At the end of a course, students are given a mark based on their assignments during the course. The marks are found to have a mean of 82 and a standard deviation of 12. The students are awarded a certificate according to these rules.

Distinction	above 110
Credit	over 90 and up to 110
Pass	over 60 and up to 90
Fail	60 or less

(a) Find the proportion of candidates awarded each type of certificate.

(b) If there are 90 students on the course, how many certificates of each type are awarded?

D Working backwards (answers p 139)

Sometimes a problem requires the normal distribution to be used 'in reverse': the probability or proportion is given and the corresponding value is required.

For example, a machine produces chocolate bars whose weight is normally distributed with mean 200 g and standard deviation 8 g. The company will not allow more than 10% of bars to be over a certain weight. They need to know where to set the limit so that only 10% are above it.

We need to find the value of z for which $\Phi(z) = 0.90$.

We could look through the table for $\Phi(z)$ to find the nearest probability to 0.90. However, since this kind of 'reverse' problem is common, a table is produced of **percentage points** of the standard normal distribution, for frequently used percentages.

For a given probability p, the percentage points table shows the value of z for which $P(Z > z) = p$.

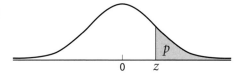

The table supplied for the AS/A2 exam is shown below (and is also on page 121).

p	z	p	z
0.5000	0.0000	0.0500	1.6449
0.4000	0.2533	0.0250	1.9600
0.3000	0.5244	0.0100	2.3263
0.2000	0.8416	0.0050	2.5758
0.1500	1.0364	0.0010	3.0902
0.1000	1.2816	0.0005	3.2905

This shows that 0.1000 (or 10%) of the area is to the right of 1.2816 (1.2816 s.d.s above the mean).

In the chocolate bars example, to ensure that only 10% of bars are above the limit, the limit must be 1.2816 standard deviations above the mean, or $200 + 1.2816 \times 8$, which is 210.3 g (to one decimal place).

Because the normal curve is symmetrical, the percentage points table can also be used for percentages or probabilities in the left-hand 'tail' of the distribution.

D1 A manufacturer fills cans with beans. The weight of beans in a can is normally distributed with mean 250 g and standard deviation 10 g. The manufacturer needs to quote a weight such that 95% of all cans contain that weight or more (so only 5% can be less than this weight). What weight should be quoted?

D2 The heights of a group of boys are known to be normally distributed with mean 174 cm and standard deviation 8 cm.
Give an interval, symmetrical about the mean, within which 90% of the heights of these boys lie.

In any problem involving the normal distribution, there are always four quantities:

- the mean of the distribution
- the standard deviation or the variance of the distribution
- a given value or values of the variable
- a probability or proportion

In any problem you will be given some of these quantities and asked to find others. The following examples show some of the variations.

Example 5

A machine produces packages with standard deviation 8 g. The mean can be adjusted to any given value. The company requires the machine to be set so that only 2.5% of packets weigh less than the weight stated on the packet, 250 g. To what mean weight must the machine be set?

Solution

Using the percentage points table as if the shaded area is in the right-hand tail, when $p = 0.0250$, $z = 1.9600$.

To have only 2.5% of packets below 250 g requires this value to be 1.96 standard deviations below the mean.

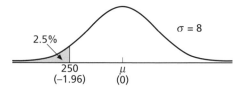

So $\mu = 250 + (1.96 \times 8) = 265.68$.

So the machine must be set to give a mean weight of 265.68 g.

Example 6

The continuous random variable X is normally distributed with mean 40.

(a) Given that $P(X < 49) = 0.7257$, find the standard deviation of X.

(b) Find the value of k such that $P(X > k) = 0.1151$.

Solution

(a) By looking for 0.7257 in the $\Phi(z)$ column of the normal distribution function table, we find that $\Phi(0.6) = 0.7257$.

So 49 is 0.6 s.d.s above the mean (40).

So $0.6\sigma = 9$, from which $\sigma = \dfrac{9}{0.6} = 15$.

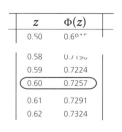

z	$\Phi(z)$
0.50	0.6915
0.58	0.7190
0.59	0.7224
0.60	0.7257
0.61	0.7291
0.62	0.7324

(b) The situation is shown in this diagram.

The unshaded area $= 1 - 0.1151 = 0.8849$.

By looking for 0.8849 in the $\Phi(z)$ column, we find that $\Phi(1.2) = 0.8849$.

So k is 1.2 s.d.s above the mean $= 40 + 1.2 \times 15$
$$= 58$$

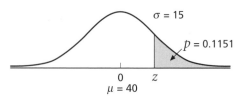

Example 7

A salmon farm has a large population of fish whose weights are known to be normally distributed. However, the mean and standard deviation of the weights are not known. A large number of fish were netted and it was found that 5% of these weighed less than 3 kg, and 2.3% weighed more than 6 kg. Use this information to estimate the mean and standard deviation of the weight of the salmon.

Solution

Sketch the details.

Using the percentage points table as if the left-hand shaded area is in a right-hand tail, when $p = 0.0500$, $z = 1.64(49)$.

At the upper tail the percentage points table is not accurate enough. However, you can search in the body of the standard normal tables. $\Phi(2.0) = 0.977(2)$

So 3 kg is 1.64 s.d.s below the mean, giving $\mu - 1.64\sigma = 3$ (1)
And 6 kg is 2 s.d.s above the mean, giving $\mu + 2\sigma = 6$ (2)

Subtract equation (1) *from* (2). $3.64\sigma = 3 \Rightarrow \sigma = 3 \div 3.64 = 0.8$
Use equation (2). $\mu + 1.6 = 6 \Rightarrow \mu = 4.4$

So the fish have an approximate mean weight 4.4 kg and standard deviation 0.8 kg.

Exercise D (answers p 139)

In each of the following questions, assume that the variable is normally distributed.

1 The marks in an examination have mean 47 and standard deviation 12. The top 15% are to be awarded an A grade. What mark must be achieved in order to gain an A grade?

2 A machine packing bags of sugar fills them with a weight whose standard deviation is 0.0025 kg. To what value should the mean weight be set so that 90% of all bags are over 1 kg in weight?

3 A machine fills bottles of oil with mean volume 265 ml and standard deviation 10 ml.

(a) What proportion of bottles are filled with less than 250 ml?

(b) An engineer claims he can reduce the standard deviation of the amount the bottles are filled with. What must the standard deviation be changed to so that 1 in 200 bottles have a volume less than 250 ml?

4 The time taken to fit a new exhaust on a car at Speedy's Exhausts was found to have mean 20 minutes and a standard deviation of 3 minutes.

(a) What is the probability of it taking less than 15 minutes to fit an exhaust?

(b) What is the fitting time that will only be exceeded on 10% of occasions?

(c) At Superfast the standard deviation of fitting times is 4 minutes. The probability of it taking more than 10 minutes to fit an exhaust at Superfast is 0.9332. What is the mean fitting time at Superfast?

5 The mean length of a species of snake is 80 cm with standard deviation 7 cm. Give an interval which is symmetrical about the mean within which 95% of the lengths of these snakes lie.

6 In an examination, 10% of candidates scored more than 70 marks and 15% scored fewer than 35 marks. Find the mean and standard deviation.

7 The continuous random variable X is normally distributed with mean μ and standard deviation σ.

Given that $P(X > 30.0) = 0.1056$ and $P(X < 21.2) = 0.2266$, find the values of μ and σ.

8 A production process making bars of chocolate rejects any bars which weigh more than 165 g as too heavy and any weighing less than 140 g as too light. In a large batch of bars 5.5% were rejected as too heavy and 11.5% as too light. Find the mean and standard deviation of the weight of the chocolate bars.

*9 A machine produces ball bearings whose mean diameter is 224 mm with standard deviation 4 mm. The machine has a filter which removes ball bearings over a certain diameter.

(a) If the largest 20% of ball bearings have been removed, what diameter has been specified?

(b) Given that the largest 20% are removed, find the median diameter of the remaining ball bearings.

The packers' rules

The normal distribution is important to manufacturers, who must meet quality control regulations.

When you buy items with a given weight or volume you may have noticed an 'e' symbol in front of the amount. This means that the amount is an 'average quantity' and companies are bound by law to follow the 'packers' rules' for this average. These state that:

• The actual contents of packages must on average be the stated amount.

• No more than 2.5% may be 'non-standard', that is less than the given amount minus the tolerable negative error (TNE). The TNE depends on the size of the packet.

• No package may be 'inadequate', that is more than two TNEs less than the stated amount.

The TNE for a packet labelled 'e125 g' is $4\frac{1}{2}$% so a manufacturer would need to make sure that only 2.5% of packets weighed less than 119.375 g (125 less 4.5%).

Weights and volumes in containers, weights of mass-produced items and other measures in manufacturing often follow a normal distribution.

Key points

- The probability distribution of a continuous random variable is represented by a graph. The area under the graph in a given interval gives the probability of a value lying in that interval. (pp 104–105)

- If a variable X follows a normal probability distribution, with mean μ and standard deviation σ, we write $X \sim N(\mu, \sigma^2)$. (p 109)

- The variable $Z = \dfrac{X - \mu}{\sigma}$ is called the standard normal variable corresponding to X. (p 108)

- Z is such that $Z \sim N(0, 1)$; $\Phi(z) = P(Z < z)$. (p 106)

- The percentage points table shows, for a probability p, the value of z such that $P(Z > z) = p$. (p 111)

Mixed questions (answers p 140)

1 The continuous random variable X is normally distributed with mean 8.5 and variance 12.25. Find $P(7.5 < X < 10)$.

2 The weight of pistachios put into bags by a machine is normally distributed with mean 265 g and standard deviation 7 g.
What minimum weight should be quoted on the packets so that only 1 in 1000 packets weigh less than this value?

3 The volume of honey that a machine pours into a jar can be modelled by a normal distribution with mean 275 ml and standard deviation 15 ml.

(a) What is the probability that the machine pours between 260 ml and 290 ml of honey into a jar?

(b) The jars have a capacity of 300 ml. What is the probability that a jar is filled with more than 300 ml of honey and so overflows?

4 (a) The diameter of a toad's blood corpuscles are thought to follow a normal distribution with mean 0.0158 mm and standard deviation 0.002 mm. What is the probability of a toad blood corpuscle having a diameter of less than 0.0155 mm?

(b) The standard deviation of a frog's blood corpuscles is also 0.002 mm. In an experiment it was found that 20% of blood corpuscles from a frog were larger than 0.0155 mm.
Find the mean diameter of a frog's blood corpuscle.

5 The continuous random variable X is normally distributed with mean μ and standard deviation σ. Given that $P(X > 11.1) = 0.0668$ and $P(X > 8.7) = 0.3085$, find the values of μ and σ.

6 A soft drinks vending machine pours the chosen drink into a cup at the press of a button. The volume of drink poured follows a normal distribution with mean 475 ml and standard deviation 20 ml.

(a) Find the probability that the volume of drink delivered will be

   (i) less than 480 ml   (ii) between 460 ml and 490 ml

(b) The cups that the drinks are poured into have a capacity of 500 ml. Find the probability that the amount of drink poured into a cup is greater than the capacity of the cup and so overflows.

(c) To reduce the problem of overflowing cups, an engineer can adjust the mean value that is poured. To what should the mean value be adjusted so that the probability of a cup overflowing is 0.001?

Test yourself (answers p 140)

1 The continuous random variable X is normally distributed with mean 8 and standard deviation 2. Find $P(7 < X < 11)$.

2 A drinks machine dispenses coffee into cups. A sign on the machine indicates that each cup contains 50 ml of coffee. The machine actually dispenses a mean amount of 55 ml per cup and 10% of the cups contain less than the amount stated on the sign. Assuming that the amount of coffee dispensed into each cup is normally distributed find

(a) the standard deviation of the amount of coffee dispensed per cup in ml

(b) the percentage of cups that contain more than 61 ml

Following complaints, the owners of the machine make adjustments. Only 2.5% of cups now contain less than 50 ml. The standard deviation of the amount dispensed is reduced to 3 ml.

Assuming that the amount of coffee dispensed is still normally distributed,

(c) find the new mean amount of coffee per cup   Edexcel

3 The continuous random variable X is normally distributed with mean 20 and standard deviation 8.

(a) Find $P(X > 24.4)$.

(b) Find the value of k given that $P(20 - k \leq X \leq 20 + k) = 0.438$.

4 A consumer protection organisation tested a large sample of batteries of a particular make and found that 5% lasted for longer than 15 hours and 10% lasted for less than 9 hours.

Assuming that the lifetimes of the batteries are normally distributed, find

(a) the mean and standard deviation of the lifetimes (to 2 d.p.)

(b) the percentage of batteries whose lifetimes are greater than 10 hours, giving your answer to the nearest 0.1%

8 Modelling

The fundamental ideas of mathematical modelling were introduced on pages 43–44. This short chapter reviews the types of model that you have met while working through this book.

Why model?

The main reason for modelling a real-world situation mathematically is to answer questions, solve problems and make reasonably confident predictions about its behaviour.

There are obvious advantages if mathematics can be used to solve a real-world problem. If, to take a very simple example, it can be shown mathematically that a petrol tank of a certain shape would have insufficient capacity, that would cut out the time, effort and expense involved in making a real tank only to find that it overflows when the required amount is poured in.

In many cases, mathematical modelling, or possibly computer simulation, is the only way to solve a problem such as, for example, getting as reliable an estimate as possible of the number of people aged over 70 ten years from now.

Statistical models

What distinguishes **statistical models** from mathematical models in general is the fact that they are used to model situations that involve **uncertainty**. Here are some examples.

Probability models

Probability models can be used to calculate the reliability of an appliance made up of components. A simple example of this type of problem appears in question 1 on page 57.

Another example where probability models are used in real life is in modelling the spread of diseases. If an infected person comes into contact with an uninfected person, the outcome is not automatic infection. It is uncertain whether the uninfected person will catch the disease. The probability of doing so is affected by the nature of the disease, the general health of the person and so on.

The values that need to be 'fed in' to a model in order to arrive at definite predictions are called **parameters**. For example, in a model of the spread of a disease, values need to be given to the probability of transmission, to the length of time before someone who has caught the disease becomes infectious themselves, and the length of time before a person is no longer infectious. These values will need to be found out, or at least estimated, through collecting data from experiments or surveys.

Regression models

If the relationship between two variables can be expressed as a mathematical equation, the equation can be used to make predictions. However, variables in the real world do not follow any mathematical relationship exactly, and this is where uncertainty enters. A linear regression line represents a best attempt to fit a line to a set of data. Any predictions made from it are uncertain.

The reliability of predictions depends on how closely the line fits the data. For example, a linear regression line can be found for all three data sets below, but in only one case is it an appropriate model.

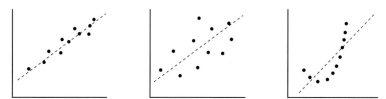

The parameters in the linear regression model are the values of a and b, the intercept and gradient which together define the position of the regression line.

One example used in practice (see page 64) is the linear regression equation for the height of a person in terms of the length of a particular bone in their body. This has been used to estimate the heights of people whose skeletal remains are discovered, thus helping to establish their identity.

Random variables: distribution models

Real world quantities can often be modelled by a random variable whose distribution is defined by a mathematical function.

As shown in chapter 6, a discrete random variable with the probability function $p(x) = \dfrac{1}{2^x}$, $x = 1, 2, 3, \ldots$ can be used to model the number of births needed before a child of a particular sex is born. There are many other discrete distributions that are used to model real processes.

The most important mathematically defined continuous distribution is the normal distribution. Many real quantities, for example the height of adult males or the errors made by measuring devices, have a distribution that can be closely modelled by the normal distribution.

The parameters which specify the normal distribution model in an individual case are the mean μ and standard deviation σ. Once these are known, other facts about the distribution can be deduced.

Checking the validity of a model

If an inappropriate model is used, then 'garbage in, garbage out' applies. Before using a particular type of model it is important to check that the assumptions it makes correspond with the situation being modelled. For example, there is no point in applying a probability model that assumes outcomes to be independent to situations where this is not the case. Many of the errors made in statistics arise from misuse of models.

Excel functions

Although current examination requirements make it necessary to practise using a calculator and statistical tables, spreadsheet functions are valuable for exploring statistical topics or dealing with large data sets.

AVERAGE(range of cells) Calculates the mean of the values in the cells, specified for example as A1:A10.

CORREL(cells for variable 1, cells for variable 2) Calculates the product moment correlation coefficient for bivariate data organised in two corresponding ranges of cells; **PEARSON** does the same (p 72).

INTERCEPT(cells for response variable, cells for explanatory variable) Calculates the y-intercept of the least squares regression line for the data organised in two corresponding ranges of cells.
SLOPE(cells for response variable, cells for explanatory variable) Calculates the gradient of the least squares regression line (the regression coefficient) (p 61).

MEDIAN(range of cells) Finds the median of the values in the stated cells.

NORMDIST(x, mean, standard deviation, TRUE) Works like the normal distribution table, except the variable does not first need to be standardised (p 106).

NORMINV($\Phi(z)$, mean, standard deviation) Works like the normal distribution table in reverse but the result is the value of the actual, not the standardised, variable. Note that the probaility used here is $\Phi(z)$, not $1 - \Phi(z)$ as in the Edexcel percentage points table (p 111).

STDEVP(range of cells) Finds the standard deviation of the values in the cells (pp 27–28).

VARP(range of cells) Finds the variance of the values in the cells (pp 26–27).

Tables

The normal distribution function

If Z is a random variable with the standard normal distribution, then $\Phi(z) = P(Z < z)$.

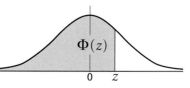

z	$\Phi(z)$	z	$\Phi(z)$	z	$\Phi(z)$	z	$\Phi(z)$	z	$\Phi(z)$
0.00	0.5000	0.50	0.6915	1.00	0.8413	1.50	0.9332	2.00	0.9772
0.01	0.5040	0.51	0.6950	1.01	0.8438	1.51	0.9345	2.02	0.9783
0.02	0.5080	0.52	0.6985	1.02	0.8461	1.52	0.9357	2.04	0.9793
0.03	0.5120	0.53	0.7019	1.03	0.8485	1.53	0.9370	2.06	0.9803
0.04	0.5160	0.54	0.7054	1.04	0.8508	1.54	0.9382	2.08	0.9812
0.05	0.5199	0.55	0.7088	1.05	0.8531	1.55	0.9394	2.10	0.9821
0.06	0.5239	0.56	0.7123	1.06	0.8554	1.56	0.9406	2.12	0.9830
0.07	0.5279	0.57	0.7157	1.07	0.8577	1.57	0.9418	2.14	0.9838
0.08	0.5319	0.58	0.7190	1.08	0.8599	1.58	0.9429	2.16	0.9846
0.09	0.5359	0.59	0.7224	1.09	0.8621	1.59	0.9441	2.18	0.9854
0.10	0.5398	0.60	0.7257	1.10	0.8643	1.60	0.9452	2.20	0.9861
0.11	0.5438	0.61	0.7291	1.11	0.8665	1.61	0.9463	2.22	0.9868
0.12	0.5478	0.62	0.7324	1.12	0.8686	1.62	0.9474	2.24	0.9875
0.13	0.5517	0.63	0.7357	1.13	0.8708	1.63	0.9484	2.26	0.9881
0.14	0.5557	0.64	0.7389	1.14	0.8729	1.64	0.9495	2.28	0.9887
0.15	0.5596	0.65	0.7422	1.15	0.8749	1.65	0.9505	2.30	0.9893
0.16	0.5636	0.66	0.7454	1.16	0.8770	1.66	0.9515	2.32	0.9898
0.17	0.5675	0.67	0.7486	1.17	0.8790	1.67	0.9525	2.34	0.9904
0.18	0.5714	0.68	0.7517	1.18	0.8810	1.68	0.9535	2.36	0.9909
0.19	0.5753	0.69	0.7549	1.19	0.8830	1.69	0.9545	2.38	0.9913
0.20	0.5793	0.70	0.7580	1.20	0.8849	1.70	0.9554	2.40	0.9918
0.21	0.5832	0.71	0.7611	1.21	0.8869	1.71	0.9564	2.42	0.9922
0.22	0.5871	0.72	0.7642	1.22	0.8888	1.72	0.9573	2.44	0.9927
0.23	0.5910	0.73	0.7673	1.23	0.8907	1.73	0.9582	2.46	0.9931
0.24	0.5948	0.74	0.7704	1.24	0.8925	1.74	0.9591	2.48	0.9934
0.25	0.5987	0.75	0.7734	1.25	0.8944	1.75	0.9599	2.50	0.9938
0.26	0.6026	0.76	0.7764	1.26	0.8962	1.76	0.9608	2.55	0.9946
0.27	0.6064	0.77	0.7794	1.27	0.8980	1.77	0.9616	2.60	0.9953
0.28	0.6103	0.78	0.7823	1.28	0.8997	1.78	0.9625	2.65	0.9960
0.29	0.6141	0.79	0.7852	1.29	0.9015	1.79	0.9633	2.70	0.9965
0.30	0.6179	0.80	0.7881	1.30	0.9032	1.80	0.9641	2.75	0.9970
0.31	0.6217	0.81	0.7910	1.31	0.9049	1.81	0.9649	2.80	0.9974
0.32	0.6255	0.82	0.7939	1.32	0.9066	1.82	0.9656	2.85	0.9978
0.33	0.6293	0.83	0.7967	1.33	0.9082	1.83	0.9664	2.90	0.9981
0.34	0.6331	0.84	0.7995	1.34	0.9099	1.84	0.9671	2.95	0.9984
0.35	0.6368	0.85	0.8023	1.35	0.9115	1.85	0.9678	3.00	0.9987
0.36	0.6406	0.86	0.8051	1.36	0.9131	1.86	0.9686	3.05	0.9989
0.37	0.6443	0.87	0.8078	1.37	0.9147	1.87	0.9693	3.10	0.9990
0.38	0.6480	0.88	0.8106	1.38	0.9162	1.88	0.9699	3.15	0.9992
0.39	0.6517	0.89	0.8133	1.39	0.9177	1.89	0.9706	3.20	0.9993
0.40	0.6554	0.90	0.8159	1.40	0.9192	1.90	0.9713	3.25	0.9994
0.41	0.6591	0.91	0.8186	1.41	0.9207	1.91	0.9719	3.30	0.9995
0.42	0.6628	0.92	0.8212	1.42	0.9222	1.92	0.9726	3.35	0.9996
0.43	0.6664	0.93	0.8238	1.43	0.9236	1.93	0.9732	3.40	0.9997
0.44	0.6700	0.94	0.8264	1.44	0.9251	1.94	0.9738	3.50	0.9998
0.45	0.6736	0.95	0.8289	1.45	0.9265	1.95	0.9744	3.60	0.9998
0.46	0.6772	0.96	0.8315	1.46	0.9279	1.96	0.9750	3.70	0.9999
0.47	0.6808	0.97	0.8340	1.47	0.9292	1.97	0.9756	3.80	0.9999
0.48	0.6844	0.98	0.8365	1.48	0.9306	1.98	0.9761	3.90	1.0000
0.49	0.6879	0.99	0.8389	1.49	0.9319	1.99	0.9767	4.00	1.0000
0.50	0.6915	1.00	0.8413	1.50	0.9332	2.00	0.9772		

Percentage points of the normal distribution

The values z in the table are those which a random variable $Z \sim N(0, 1)$ exceeds with probability p; that is, $P(Z > z) = 1 - \Phi(z) = p$.

p	z	p	z
0.5000	0.0000	0.0500	1.6449
0.4000	0.2533	0.0250	1.9600
0.3000	0.5244	0.0100	2.3263
0.2000	0.8416	0.0050	2.5758
0.1500	1.0364	0.0010	3.0902
0.1000	1.2816	0.0005	3.2905

Answers

1 Organising data

A Organising data by grouping (p 6)

A1 Less; there is more data in the upper rows of the diagram.

A2 (a)

	Paper 1		Paper 2
	6 4 1	2	3 5
	9 9 7 5 3 3	3	0 4 7 7
	8 7 5 4 2 2 0	4	0 1 1 2 5 8
	6 6 4 3 0	5	2 4 4 5 5 7 9
	8 5 2 0	6	3 4 5 5 7
		7	1

(b) Paper 1; there are more low marks (in the 20s, 30s and 40s).

A3 It makes it look as if there are more cars exceeding 60 m.p.h. than in the previous chart.

Exercise A (p 9)

1 (a)

3	2 7
4	0 3 3 5 6 8
5	2 4 4 5 7 9 9
6	3 5 6 6 7
7	2 4 8
8	3 4

(b) 32% (c) 72

2

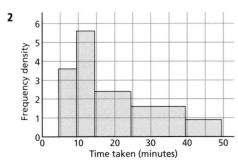

3

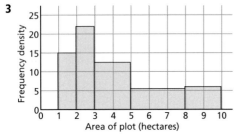

4 (a) 200 (b) 225 (c) 250 (d) 4.2°

B Organising data by ordering (p 11)

B1 Before: $Q_1 = 32$ m.p.h., $Q_3 = 56$ m.p.h.
After: $Q_1 = 30$ m.p.h., $Q_3 = 51$ m.p.h.

B2 (a) Median = 48.5, $Q_1 = 43.5$, $Q_3 = 60$
(b) Median = 59, $Q_1 = 52$, $Q_3 = 66$
(c) Median = 37, $Q_1 = 25$, $Q_3 = 48$
(d) Median = 38.5, $Q_1 = 31$, $Q_3 = 44$

B3 (a) 49 (b) 37 (c) 58 (d) 21

B4 It is the length of the box.

B5

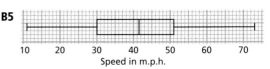

B6 For example: the median is higher on paper 2; the top half of the class is more spread out on paper 1; the marks are more evenly distributed o paper 2; the interquartile range is greater on paper 2.

Exercise B (p 14)

1 50.55 kg

2 $Q_1 = 29$, $Q_2 = 35$, $Q_3 = 43$
Interquartile range = 14

3 (a) $Q_1 = 7$ min, $Q_2 = 17.5$ min, $Q_3 = 28$ min
(b) 21 min

4 1.5, 2.5, 1.875, 0.71

5 (a)

3	3 5 7 9
4	0 3 3 4 6 7 7 9
5	0 0 1 2 4 5 5 7 8 8
6	0 7 9
7	3 7
8	0 5

(b) $Q_1 = 44$, $Q_2 = 51$, $Q_3 = 58$
(c) 80, 85
(d)

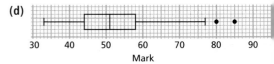

(e) The range of marks was broadly similar (apart from the two outlying high results in the first school). In the first school, half of the pupils scored between 44 and 58, but in the second the marks were distributed more widely within the range.

C Linear interpolation (p 16)

C1 8.5 minutes

Exercise C (p 17)

1 6.6 minutes

2 With fertiliser: 135.7 g
Without fertiliser: 116.7 g
The onions in the treated plot had a median weight about 19 g greater.

3 $Q_1 = 30.75$ kg, $Q_2 = 35.75$ kg, $Q_3 = 40.5$ kg

D Large data sets: percentiles (p 18)

D1 7 cm

Exercise D (p 19)

1 (a) 8.0 days   (b) 14.6 days

2 (a)

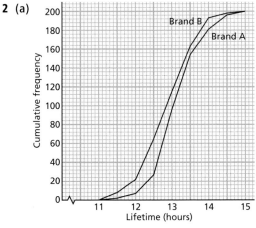

(b) Brand A: 13.03 hours
Brand B: 12.85 hours

(c) Brand A: 1.66 hours
Brand B: 1.85 hours
Brand A lifetimes are less widely spread than Brand B, now that outliers are ignored.

Test yourself (p 21)

1 (a) $Q_1 = 29$, $Q_2 = 38$, $Q_3 = 47$

(b) The median has fallen slightly.
The interquartile range has increased so the number of passengers is slightly more variable.

2 (a) 45 is an outlier; 127 is not.

(b)

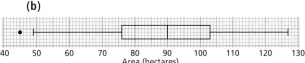

3 (a)

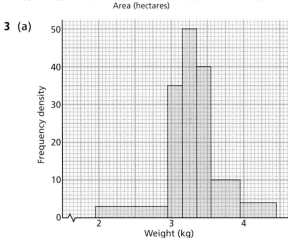

(b) 3.3 kg

4 (a) $Q_1 = 30$ lengths, $Q_2 = 42$ lengths, $Q_3 = 46$ lengths

(b)

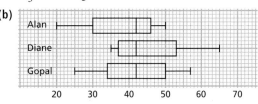

(c) All three swimmers have the same median, 42. However, Alan never swims many more lengths than this and Diane never swims many fewer. Another way of saying this is that Alan's distances are negatively skewed while Diane's distances are positively skewed. Gopal's distances are fairly symmetrically distributed about the median. However, the spread (whether measured by the range or the interquartile range) is similar in all three cases.

2 Summarising data

A Measures of average (p 22)

A1 (a) Median = 13.5, mean = 14

(b) (i) Median: none; mean: increases by 1

(ii) Median: none; mean: increases by 2

(iii) Median: none; mean: decreases by 1.3

A2 (a) 25.5

(b) (i) It increases by 20 (to become 45.5).

(ii) It is doubled (51).

(iii) It is doubled and then increased by 20 (71).

(iv) It is multiplied by 3 and then decreased by 10 (66.5).

A3 (a) 9.5   (b) 395

A4 21.72

A5 For example, new value = (original value − 21) × 10

A6 (a) 54, 29, 106, 38, 60, 49   (b) 56   (c) 35.6

Exercise A (p 24)

1 (a) 6

(b) (i) 46   (ii) 260   (iii) 1   (iv) 180   (v) 187

2 £279.29

3 9.7 cm

4 16 372 miles

5 $32.4 \times 13.8 \neq 491.6$

B Measures of spread (p 25)

B1 The lengths of leaves inside appear to have a wider spread.

B2 The deviations are
0.8, −1.0, 0.1, −1.1, 0.7, 0.4, −0.8, 1.0, 0.2, 0.3, −0.6
The sum of the deviations is zero.

B3 The deviations are
1.5, −0.6, 0.3, −1.3, 0.1, −0.4, 0.4
and these sum to zero as well. This will always happen since the mean is always such that the total of the deviations from it is zero. The mean can be thought of as a 'centre of gravity'.

B4 The sums of squared deviations are
Outside: 5.64
Inside: 4.72
This is not a useful measure as there is a different number of leaves in each set.

B5 The variances are
Outside: 0.513
Inside: 0.674
This suggests the inside group has the greater spread.

B6 The standard deviations are
Outside: 0.716 cm
Inside: 0.821 cm

B7 Mean = 3 years, s.d. = 1.69 years

B8 Mean = 2.7, s.d. = 1.68

Exercise B (p 28)

1 Mean = 6 peas, s.d. = 2.45 peas

2 Mean = 51 kg, s.d. = 2.19 kg

3 Mean = $\frac{1245}{25}$ = 49.8 kg

s.d. = $\sqrt{\dfrac{62\,820}{25} - 49.8^2}$ = 5.72 kg

4 (a) Mean = $\frac{85.6}{10}$ = 8.56 cm

s.d. = $\sqrt{\dfrac{742.96}{10} - 8.56^2}$ = 1.01 cm

(b) Corrected $\sum h = 85.6 - 6.8 + 8.6 = 87.4$
$\sum h^2 = 742.96 - 6.8^2 + 8.6^2 = 770.68$
This gives the correct mean as 8.74 cm and the s.d. as 0.825 cm.

5 (a) 3 May: $\mu = 14.8\,°C$, $\sigma = 1.66\,°C$
10 May: $\mu = 18.8\,°C$, $\sigma = 1.47\,°C$

(b) The temperature on 10 May was higher (on average) than on 3 May. There was less variation around the country on 10 May.

6 x: $\mu = 38.5$, $\sigma = 12.0$
   y: $\mu = 45.3$, $\sigma = 7.0$

The mean journey time is only about 7 minutes longer by the country lanes and it is much more predictable.

C Scaling and coding (p 29)

C1 4.58; they are spread out in the same way as the first set.

C2 9.16; they are twice as spread out.

C3 $\mu = 16.0$ years, $\sigma = 0.25$ years

C4 $\mu = 162.5$, $\sigma = 42$

C5 $\mu = 53.6\,°\text{F}$, $\sigma = 0.9\,°\text{F}$

C6 (a) 7, 18, 11, 28, 5, 10, 4, 29
   (b) Calculation leading to mean $= 14$
   (c) Calculation leading to $\Sigma y^2 = 2260$
   (d) 9.3
   (e) 19.4 °C
   (f) (i) None   (ii) It is multiplied by 10.
   (g) 0.93 °C

C7 (a) 10, 2, 4, 17, 13, −6, 6
   (b) $\mu = 6.57$, $\sigma = 7.05$
   (c) $\mu = 81.57\,\text{kg}$, $\sigma = 7.05\,\text{kg}$

C8 (a) $\mu = 7.3$, $\sigma = 3.26$
   (b) $\mu = £273\,000$, $\sigma = £32\,600$

C9 (a) 4970   (b) $\mu = 5093$, $\sigma = 85.4$

Exercise C (p 32)

1 $\mu = 185.24$ pounds, $\sigma = 14.41$ pounds

2 $\mu = 2.52$ ohms, $\sigma = 0.765$ ohms

3 $\mu = 62.5$, $\sigma = 18.3$

4 $\mu = 1012.75$ millibars, $\sigma = 10.0$ millibars

5 (a) 9, 39, 90, 139, 239, 439, 465, 639, 710
   (b) $\mu = 307.67$, $\sigma = 248.46$
   (c) $\mu = £5338$, $\sigma = £1242$

6 $\mu = 103$ seconds, $\sigma = 11.7$ seconds

7 (a) 42, −30, −65, −84, 28, −31, −15, 107, 25, 10

(b) $\mu = -1.3$, $\sigma = 53.0$

(c) $\mu = 49.87\,\text{s}$, $\sigma = 5.30\,\text{s}$

(d) $\mu = 49.35$, $\sigma = 26.5$

8 (a) $\mu = 23.4\,\text{m}$, $\sigma = 6.8\,\text{m}$
   (b) $\mu = 17.2\,\text{m}$, $\sigma = 8.3\,\text{m}$
   (c) The oak trees are generally taller and less spread out in height.

9 (a) $\mu = £31\,400$, $\sigma = £5127$
   (b) $\mu = £22\,562.50$, $\sigma = £2124$
   (c) The experts were much closer in agreement and valued the painting much less highly.

D Working with frequency distributions (p 34)

D1 (a) (i) 47   (ii) 167
   (b) 2.35   (c) 1.68

D2 (a) 50   (b) 120, 400   (c) $\mu = 2.4$, $\sigma = 1.50$

D3 73.5 kg

Exercise D (p 35)

1 (a) 7.5, 17.5, 22.5, 27.5, 32.5
   (b) Morning: $\mu \approx 20.5$ min, $\sigma \approx 6.39$ min
       Afternoon: $\mu \approx 15.5$ min, $\sigma \approx 6.03$ min
   (c) Morning calls are on average longer. There is not much difference in the variation in the length of calls.

2 (a) Using mid-interval values 7, 22, … gives mean $= 28.63$ min, s.d. $= 16.80$ min
   (b) There are few groups. A more accurate result could have been obtained using smaller group intervals.

3 (a) Mean $= 23.3$ words, s.d. $= 11.2$ words
   (b) Most of the sentences are in the middle three groups so the group intervals may be too large. Since the distribution is asymmetrical it may not be safe to use the assumption that the data is evenly spread in each group.

4 (a) Before coaching: $\mu \approx 11.1$, $\sigma \approx 9.2$
       After coaching: $\mu \approx 23.3$, $\sigma \approx 12.5$
   (b) The mean length of a rally has greatly increased although there is slightly more variation in the length.

E Skewness (p 37)

E1 (a) Paper A: median = 55, mean = 54.5; σ = 11.35
Paper B: median = 58, mean = 57.1; σ = 10.43

(b) Paper A: –0.041, paper B: –0.086

(c) The results are better on paper B and slightly more uniform. The marks on both papers are negatively skewed, more so for paper B.

F Choosing and using measures of average and spread (p 38)

F1 (a) (i) £25 000   (ii) £30 536

(b) The median

F2 (a) We have no idea of the maximum time taken.

(b) Median = 56, interquartile range = 40

Mixed questions (p 40)

1 (a) Gauge A: μ = 2.79, σ = 0.114
Gauge B: μ = 2.5, σ = 0.253

(b) Gauge A is much more consistent. The error in the mean could be corrected by adjusting the scale or by subtracting from measured readings but the inconsistency of B cannot be compensated for.

2 (a) μ = 41.2, σ = 10

(b) $\sum x$ = 958, $\sum x^2$ = 37 016

(c) μ = 38.32, σ = 3.50

3 (a) Mean $\approx$ 63.75, 63.75 – 65 = –1.25

(b) Mean $\approx$ 48.75, negative (48.75 – 50 = –1.25)

(c) Although (mean – median) is the same for both distributions, the first box plot appears to have a greater negative skew. This raises a doubt about the reliability of the (mean – median) formula.

4 (a) 50   (b) 50

(c) 159.9 cm   (d) 163 cm

(e) Negatively skewed

(f) They assume that the heights of the girls in each interval are reasonably evenly spread within the interval.

Test yourself (p 42)

1 (a)

(b) Median $\approx$ £229, IQR $\approx$ £312

(c) μ = £308, σ = £258

(d) It might be argued that using the median and interquartile range removes the uncertainty about how the five largest values are distributed in the wide interval 1000–1500 though in fact their effect is slight. In practice most businesses comparing one year with another do so using total sales, so would not throw away data by grouping. Here nearly half the values lie in the lowest interval, 1–200; the assumption that these values are uniformly distributed in this interval (on which the estimated mean and lower quartile both depend) is not a safe one.

2 (a) Median = 33, IQR = 24

(b)

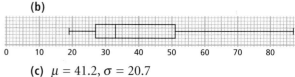

(c) μ = 41.2, σ = 20.7

(d)

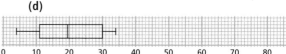

(e) The male doctors deliver more babies on average. Although the number delivered by male doctors is highly variable, the distribution is positively skewed, with few delivering the highest numbers.

3 Probability

A Modelling (p 43)

A1 The proportion should converge to 0.7 $\left(\frac{25}{36}\right)$.

A2 The situation can be modelled with two dice taking, say, a score of 4 or more to represent 'the component is working'. The probability of the appliance working is $1 - \frac{1}{2} \times \frac{1}{2}$, which is $\frac{3}{4}$.

B Outcomes and events (p 45)

B1 12

B2 13

B3 From left to right: 30, 9, 10

B4 22

B5 (a) 40   (b) 39

B6 $P(C') = \frac{10}{13}$

$P(C') = \frac{10}{13} = 1 - \frac{3}{13} = 1 - P(C)$

A and A' together account for all possible outcomes.
So $P(A) + P(A') = 1 \Rightarrow P(A') = 1 - P(A)$

B7 (a) (i) $\frac{3}{52}$ (ii) $\frac{22}{52} = \frac{11}{26}$

(b) $P(C) + P(D) - P(C \cap D)$

$= \frac{12}{52} + \frac{13}{52} - \frac{3}{52}$

$= \frac{22}{52} = P(C \cup D)$

(c)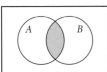

If $P(A)$ and $P(B)$ are added, then $P(A \cap B)$ is included twice.
So $P(A \cup B) = P(A) + P(B) - P(A \cap B)$

B8 (a) 0   (b) $P(A \cup B) = P(A) + P(B)$

Exercise B (p 48)

1 (a) $\frac{1}{5}$ (b) $\frac{3}{20}$ (c) $\frac{2}{5}$

---

2 (a)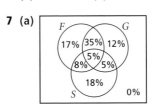

(b) (i) 0.3   (ii) 0.25

3 (a) 0.35   (b) 0.4   (c) 0.25

4 (a) 0.41   (b) 0.05   (c) 0.59

5 (a) 0.6   (b) 0.5   (c) 0.2

6 (a) 0.09   (b) 0.46   (c) 0.54   (d) 0.87

7 (a)

F G
17% 35% 12%
5%
8% 5%
18%
S 0%

(b) (i) 0.17   (ii) 0.26

C Conditional probability (p 49)

C1 (a) $\frac{5}{12}$ (b) $\frac{1}{2}$ (c) $\frac{1}{6}$

C2 $\dfrac{P(L \cap E)}{P(E)} = \dfrac{\frac{1}{6}}{\frac{1}{2}} = \frac{1}{6} \times 2 = \frac{1}{3}$

C3 (a) The probability that the number is even, given that it is less than 6

(b) $\frac{2}{5}$

C4 (a) $\frac{2}{3}$ (b) $\frac{1}{2}$ (c) $\frac{1}{5}$ (d) $\frac{1}{8}$

C5 (a)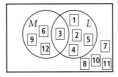

(b) (i) $\frac{1}{5}$ (ii) $\frac{1}{4}$

Exercise C (p 50)

1 (a) $\frac{4}{7}$ (b) $\frac{2}{3}$

2 (a) 0.6   (b) 0.4   (c) 0.28

3 (a)

picture map
27% 3% 7%
63%

(b) 0.1   (c) 0.3   (d) 0.63   (e) 0.9

4 (a) $\frac{3}{8}$ **(b)** $\frac{2}{7}$

5 (a) 0.4   **(b)** $\frac{2}{3}$ **(c)** 0.8

6 (a) $P(S\,|\,T') = \dfrac{P(S\cap T')}{P(T')}$

Substituting the values given,

$0.2 = \dfrac{P(S\cap T')}{0.45}$

$\Rightarrow P(S\cap T') = 0.09$

By considering a Venn diagram,

$P(S\cap T) = P(S) - P(S\cap T')$

$\quad = 0.45 - 0.09 = 0.36$

(b) 0.8

7 (a)

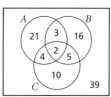

(b) 0.61   **(c)** 0.21   **(d)** 0.47   **(e)** $\frac{21}{47} = 0.45$

D Independent events (p 51)

D1 (a) (i) $\frac{1}{3}$ **(ii)** $\frac{1}{2}$ **(iii)** $\frac{1}{3}$ **(iv)** $\frac{1}{2}$

(b) $P(M\,|\,E) = P(M)$ and $P(E\,|\,M) = P(E)$

Each conditional probability is equal to the probability without the condition. So E and M are independent.

Exercise D (p 52)

1 (a) $\frac{130}{200} = 0.65$

(b) $\frac{72}{120} = 0.6$

(c) P(maths\,|\,male) and P(maths) are not equal. So studying maths is not independent of the gender.

Alternatively: P(maths) = 0.65, P(male) = 0.6

P(maths and male) = 0.36

As $0.65 \times 0.6 \neq 0.36$, the events are not independent.

2 (a) 0.12   **(b)** 0.58

3 (a) (i) $\frac{1}{6}$ **(ii)** $\frac{1}{2}$ **(iii)** $\frac{1}{3}$

(b) They are because $P(A\cap B) = P(A)\times P(B)$

4 (a) 0.2   **(b)** 0.5   **(c)** 0.1   **(d)** 0.6

5 $P(A\cap B) = 0.8 + 0.45 - 0.89 = 0.36$

$\quad P(A)P(B) = 0.36$

6 (a) (i) $x + y + z = 0.84$ **(ii)** $\dfrac{y}{y+z} = 0.6$

      (iii) $\dfrac{y}{x+y} = 0.75$

(b) 0.56

(c) They are not because

P(A) = 0.56 and P(A\,|\,B) = 0.6,

so $P(A) \neq P(A\,|\,B)$.

(d) (i) 0.7   **(ii)** 0.42

7 (a) 0.52   **(b)** 0.65

(c) $P(S)P(T) = 0.8\times 0.65 = 0.52 = P(S\cap T)$

E Tree diagrams (p 53)

E1 (a)

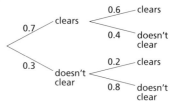

(b) (i) 0.42   **(ii)** 0.28   **(iii)** 0.06   **(iv)** 0.2

(c) (i) 0.76   **(ii)** 0.34

E2 (a) $\frac{3}{5}$ **(b)** $\frac{1}{2}$ **(c)** $\frac{3}{4}$

(d)

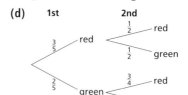

(i) $\frac{3}{10}$ **(ii)** $\frac{3}{5}$ **(iii)** $\frac{1}{10}$

E3 (a) $\frac{1}{20}$ **(b)** $\frac{1}{5}$

Exercise E (p 55)

1

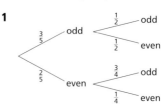

P(one odd, one even) = $\frac{3}{5}$

2 $\frac{4}{5}$

3 The first method assumes the choices are independent (that the same person can be chosen again).

Both methods only include one branch of the tree; they assume the girls must be chosen before the boy.

The correct probability is $\frac{1}{2}$.

4 (a) (i) 0.6   **(ii)** 0.225

   (b) $\frac{7}{31} = 0.226$

5 (a)

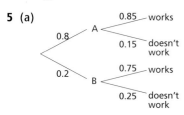

   (b) 0.83   **(c)** 0.294

6 (a) 0.275   **(b)** 0.345

Mixed questions (p 57)

1 (a) 0.126   **(b)** 0.0984

2 $P(A \cap B) = P(A)P(B|A) = 0.42$
$P(B) = P(A \cup B) - P(A) + P(A \cap B) = 0.6$
$P(A)P(B) = 0.42 = P(A \cap B)$

3 (a) (i) $\frac{216}{343}$ **(ii)** $\frac{108}{343}$

   (b) $\frac{30}{49}$

Test yourself (p 58)

1 (a) 0.075   **(b)** 0.475   **(c)** 0.25

2 (a) 0.28   **(b)** 0.3

   (c)

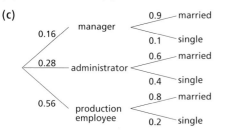

   (d) 0.76   **(e)** 0.59

3 (a) (i) $\frac{2}{5}$ **(ii)** 0   **(iii)** $\frac{9}{10}$ **(iv)** 0

   (b) (i) They are, because
$$P(A \cup B) = \frac{9}{10} = P(A) + P(B)$$

     (ii) They are not: $P(A \cap B) = 0$; $P(A)P(B) = \frac{1}{5}$; so $P(A \cap B) \neq P(A)P(B)$

4 (a) $P(A \cap B) = P(A)P(B|A)$
$$= \frac{1}{2} \times \frac{11}{12}$$
$$= \frac{11}{24}$$

   (b)

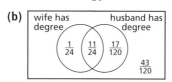

   (c) $\frac{11}{60}$ **(d)** $\frac{43}{120}$ **(e)** $\frac{49}{144}$

There is an assumption made in the above solution to (e) that taking out one couple from the club does not alter the probabilities when the second couple is taken. If the club is 'large', then taking out one couple will not significantly alter the probabilities. Because the probability that the husband but not the wife has a degree is $\frac{17}{120}$, it follows that there must be at least 120 couples in the club, which is large enough to justify the approximation.

4 Linear regression

A The least squares regression line (p 59)

A1 The scatter diagram shows that as the height of the ramp increases, the distance the car travels also increases in a linear fashion.

A2 (a) A line of best fit on the scatter diagram

(b) An equation close to $y = 4x + 25$

(c) $\bar{x} = 25$, $\bar{y} = 125$

A3 The line $y = 3x + 50$ plotted on the scatter diagram

A4

Height	5	10	15	20	25	30	35	40	45
Actual	40	44	106	91	175	138	169	175	187
Predicted	65	80	95	110	125	140	155	170	185
d_i	−25	−36	11	−19	50	−2	14	5	2

$$\sum d_i = 0$$

A5 $\sum d_i^2 = 5132$

A6

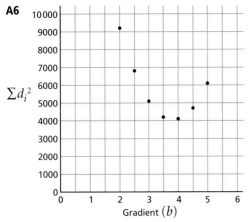

Gradient (b)

The optimum gradient is about 3.85.

A7 (a) $\sum x = 225$ $\sum y = 1125$
$\sum xy = 33\,895$ $\sum x^2 = 7125$

(b) $S_{xy} = 33\,895 - \dfrac{225 \times 1125}{9} = 5770$

$S_{xx} = 7125 - \dfrac{225^2}{9} = 1500$

(c) 3.847

(d) $a = 28.833$, $y = 28.833 + 3.847x$

(e) The line on the scatter diagram

A8 (a) 94.3 cm (b) 40.4 cm (c) 259 cm

Exercise A (p 62)

1 (a) (i) 2.199 (ii) $S_{xx} = 3.3$
(iii) 0.666 (iv) 0.069

(b) $y = 0.069 + 0.666x$

2 (a)

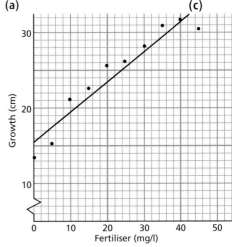

Yes, linear regression is appropriate.

(b) $y = 15.5 + 0.4x$

(c) The line as above

(d) (i) 24.3 cm (ii) 16.7 cm (iii) 35.5 cm

(e) The first two estimates are reliable as they are within the range of the data. The other value is extrapolated and therefore not as reliable.

3 (a)

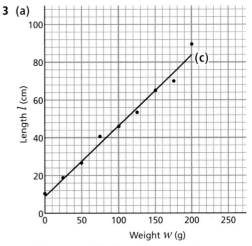

Yes, a straight line is appropriate.

(b) $l = 9.32 + 0.374w$

(c) The line on the scatter diagram, as above

(d) (i) 31.8 cm   **(ii)** 121.5 cm

(e) The value 300 g is outside the range of data. The actual value for 200 g is noticeably above the line so predicting for high values may be unreliable.

4 (a) The fuel economy is dependent on the engine size, rather than the other way around.

(b) $f = 56.805 - 10.687s$

(c) 3.37 m.p.g. This value is extrapolated beyond the range of the data and fuel economy this poor is unlikely.

B Explanatory variables

Exercise B (p 65)

1 (a) $y = 26.2x - 344$

(b) 180 ice creams

(c) The estimated additional ice cream sales for every degree rise in temperature

2 (a) Distance is the explanatory variable and time is the response variable.

(b)

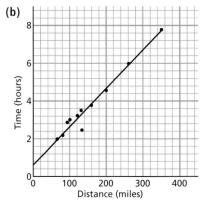

(c) $y = 0.568 + 0.0205x$, a line plotted as above.

(d) Intercept a is a fixed time (just over half an hour) added on to each journey; this might be the time taken to load and unload vehicle.

(e) Gradient b is the average time taken to travel a mile on the salesman's journeys.

(f) (i) 4.3 hours   **(ii)** 1.6 hours

    (iii) 9.2 hours

(g) (ii) is likely to be reliable, but (i) and (iii) may not be reliable because they are out of the range of the data.

3 (a)

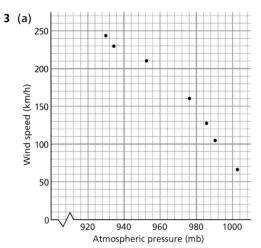

(b) $b = -2.35$, $a = 2437$

    $y = -2.35x + 2437$

(c) b tells you that for every 1 millibar increase in pressure, the predicted wind speed will drop by 2.35 km/h.

(d) (i) 322 km/h   **(ii)** −383 km/h

    (iii) 204.5 km/h

(e) The estimate for 950 millibars is the only reliable one as the others are outside the range of the original data. In fact the estimate for 1200 millibars is an impossible one.

C Coding (p 66)

C1 (a) $S_{uv} = 234.5$, $S_{uu} = 17.5$

    $v = \frac{1}{3} + 13.4u$

(b) $y = 1.340x - 0.179$

C2 $y = 0.032x - 9.84$

Exercise C (p 67)

1 (a) The top speed will be affected by the engine size, rather than the other way around.

(b)

x	0	2	3	5	7	12	17	20	22	23
y	2	6	17	21	37	44	49	59	74	81

(c)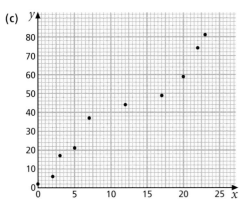

(d) Yes

(e) $y = 5.268 + 3.04x$

(f) $s = 30.4e + 65.76$

2 (a)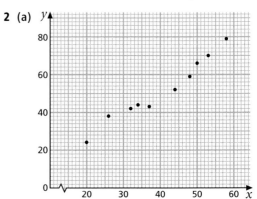

(b) Yes

(c) $y = 1.266 + 0.538x$

(d) $p = 0.538f - 21.76$

3 (a) $v = 1.019 + 1.135u$

(b) $y = 1.135x - 5.716$

(c) An estimate of the reading on the student's thermometer when the actual temperature is 0 °C; however this is not a reliable estimate as 0 °C is outside the range of values for which the thermometer was tested.

(d) 100 °C is outside the range of values for which the thermometer was tested.

Test yourself (p 68)

1 (a)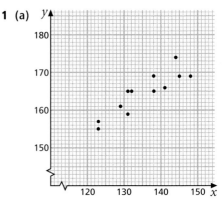

A linear model is suitable.

(b) $y = 84.133 + 0.594x$

(c) 173 cm; this estimate is not wholly reliable, as 150 cm is outside the range of data collect

2 (a)

x is the explanatory variable as advertising m affect sales, not the other way around.

(b) $y = 1.327x - 1.632$ **(c)** $c = 2657 + 13.27p$

(d) a is an estimate of the number of cars that, according to the model, would be sold with advertising spending. However $p = 0$ is a lon way outside the range of data collected so th is an extremely unreliable estimate.

(e) 27 extra. This estimate is within the range of data collected. However the model assumes that only the current advertising campaign affects sales, not the cumulative effect of rece years' campaigns. It also ignores inflation.

3 (a) $h = 217.32 - 3.090s$

(b) Each extra revolution per minute reduces the life of the drill by 3 hours.

(c) 124.6 hours

5 Correlation

A Measuring correlation (p 70)

A1 Set 1: snails

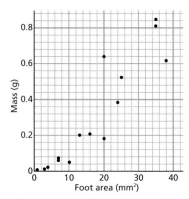

This suggests that snails with larger foot areas weigh more.

Set 2: coins

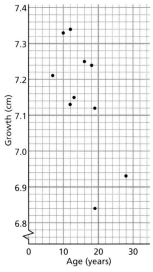

This suggests that generally older coins weigh less, although the relationship is weak.

Set 3: reactions

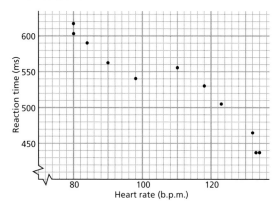

This suggests that with a higher heart rate they generally have a shorter reaction time.

Set 4: blood pressure

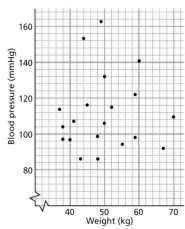

This suggests that there is little relationship between blood pressure and weight.

A2 (a) +   (b) +   (c) +

A3 B −, C +, D −

A4 (a) Since all the values will be positive the product will be a high positive value.

(b) Since all the values will be negative the product will be a high negative value.

(c) Since some values will be positive and others negative, they will cancel each other so the product will be close to zero.

Exercise A (p 73)

1 0.911; there is a strong positive correlation.

2 (a) −0.823

(b) Yes, there is a strong negative correlation.

B Scaling and coding

Exercise B (p 75)

1 (a)

a	−9	2	3	9	−1	12	5
b	−11	−2	0	5	−4	4	1

13	−1	10	7	3	1	−4	−5
0	−3	−1	2	2	0	−3	−6

(b) $\Sigma x = 45, \Sigma y = -16, \Sigma x^2 = 715, \Sigma y^2 = 246, \Sigma xy = 252$

(c) $\bar{x} = 3, \ \bar{y} = -1.067$
$a = 33$ and $b = 38.9$, so judge B's scores were generally higher.

(d) $S_{xx} = 580, S_{yy} = 228.93, S_{xy} = 300$

(e) 0.823

(f) (i) 0.823   **(ii)** Strong positive correlation

(g) It will remain the same.

2 (a) −0.809   **(b)** −0.809

(c) There is strong negative correlation between age and price.

C Interpreting correlation (p 76)

C1 No, the two variables are strongly correlated but it is not likely that one causes the other. The older students are likely to be taller and better at general knowledge than the younger ones.

C2 (a) $r = 0.909$ **(b)** $r = 0.617$

(c) When the teacher's values are included there is strong positive correlation. Without them the correlation is weaker.

Exercise C (p 77)

1 (a) $r = 0.215$

(b)

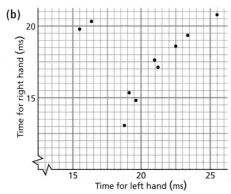

(c) A and H

(d) $r = 0.965$

(e) There is clearly a strong correlation between left- and right-handed reaction times for the right-handed students. The two left-handed students cause the correlation for the group a whole to be significantly less.

2 The correlation coefficient suggests that towns with large cinema audiences have high crime levels but this does not signify a causal link. Both variables are probably linked to a third variable such as the size of the town: bigger town are likely to have more cinemas and more crime committed.

3 (a) $r = -0.230$
This suggests that there is only a very weak correlation between temperature and the amount of electricity used.

(b)

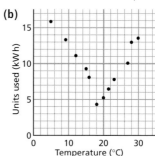

(c) The relationship between the two variables is clearly not linear.

D Correlation and regression

Exercise D (p 79)

1 (a) 0.952, yes

(b) $t = 13.295 + 8.206n$

(c) 588 min = 9 h 48 min

2 (a) −0.725

(b) −0.725

(c) There is a reasonably strong negative correlation

(d) $y = 42.248 - 1.386x$

(e) $s = 17.540 - 0.139p$

(f) Bleep score ≈ 7

3 (a) 0.825

(b) Yes, as there is a strong positive correlation between x and y (and hence a and p).

(c) $y = 7.262 + 1.196x$

(d) $p = 79.434 + 1.196a$

(e) (i) 151 mmHg

(ii) This should be fairly accurate as the correlation is strong and the age of the patient is within the range of data collected.

Test yourself (p 80)

1 (a) $S_{xy} = -157.86$, $S_{xx} = 155.92$, $S_{yy} = 214.96$

(b) −0.862

(c) (i) −0.862

(ii) Strong negative correlation, indicating that when one station's sales are high the other's are low. This could be because the total demand for petrol along this road is fairly constant from day to day.

2 (a) $S_{xx} = -12.550\,01$, $S_{xy} = -33.625\,68$, $S_{yy} = -170.906\,24$

(b) −0.726

(c) It shows reasonably strong negative correlation.

(d) $a = -0.133$, $b = 2.679$

(e) a is an estimate of the cost in £000 of reconditioning an incinerator which hasn't been used since its last reconditioning; we could expect it to be not much more than zero.

(f) (i) £6297   **(ii)** £4019

(g) 4500 hours lies significantly outside the range of data collected.

3 (a) $t = 0.880 + 1.1951s$

(b) $y = 1.195x + 13.709$

(c) 0.943; as the transformation of variables is linear the correlation relationship between them does not change.

6 Discrete random variables

A Probability functions (p 82)

A1 1

A2

x	1	2	3
$P(X = x)$	$\frac{1}{2}$	$\frac{1}{3}$	$\frac{1}{6}$

A3

y	0	1	2
$P(Y = y)$	$\frac{1}{4}$	$\frac{23}{36}$	$\frac{1}{9}$

Exercise A (p 83)

1 (a) P(square) = 0.6, P(triangle) = 0.4

(b) $P(X = 1) = 0.48$, $P(X = 2) = 0.36$, $P(X = 3) = 0.16$

x	1	2	3
$P(X = x)$	0.48	0.36	0.16

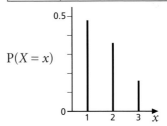

2 (a)

x	0	1	2	3
$P(X = x)$	$\frac{1}{4}$	$\frac{1}{4}$	$\frac{1}{4}$	$\frac{1}{4}$

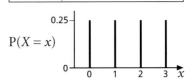

(b) Uniform

3 (a)

	1st dice					
	1	2	3	4	5	6
1	0	1	2	3	4	5
2	1	0	1	2	3	4
3	2	1	0	1	2	3
4	3	2	1	0	1	2
5	4	3	2	1	0	1
6	5	4	3	2	1	0

(2nd dice on vertical axis)

(b)

d	0	1	2	3	4	5
$P(D = d)$	$\frac{6}{36}$	$\frac{10}{36}$	$\frac{8}{36}$	$\frac{6}{36}$	$\frac{4}{36}$	$\frac{2}{36}$

(c)

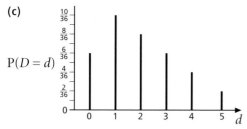

$$P(D = d)$$

(d) The game is unfair.

A possible alternative rule is 'I win if the difference is 2, 3 or 4. You win if it is 0, 1 or 5.'

4

s	0	1	2	3
P(S = s)	$\frac{125}{216}$	$\frac{25}{216}$	$\frac{30}{216}$	$\frac{36}{216}$

B Formulae for probability functions (p 84)

B1 $\sum P(X = x) = 1$ for any distribution as the probabilities must always sum to 1.

B2 $\frac{3}{18}, \frac{4}{18}, \frac{5}{18}, \frac{6}{18}$; sum = 1

B3 Since $\sum P(X = x) = \frac{21}{20}$ this cannot be the probability function of a discrete random variable.

B4 (a)

x	1	2	3	4	5
P(X = x)	$\frac{3}{5}$	$\frac{2}{5}$	$\frac{1}{5}$	0	$-\frac{1}{5}$

(b) $\sum P(X = x) = 1$

(c) This cannot be the function of a discrete random variable since P(X = 5) is negative.

Exercise B (p 86)

1

x	1	2	3	4	5
P(X = x)	$\frac{1}{15}$	$\frac{2}{15}$	$\frac{1}{5}$	$\frac{4}{15}$	$\frac{1}{3}$

$\frac{1}{15} + \frac{2}{15} + \frac{1}{5} + \frac{4}{15} + \frac{1}{3} = \frac{15}{15} = 1$

2

x	1	2	3	4
p(x)	$\frac{1}{5}$	$\frac{3}{10}$	$\frac{3}{10}$	$\frac{1}{5}$

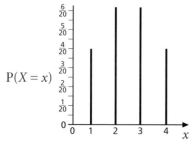

$$P(X = x)$$

3 (a)

x	1	2	3	4
P(X = x)	k	4k	9k	16k

(b) $k + 4k + 9k + 16k = 30k = 1$ so $k = \frac{1}{30}$

(c) $P(X \geq 3) = \frac{9}{30} + \frac{16}{30} = \frac{25}{30} = \frac{5}{6}$

4

x	1	2	3	4
P(X = x)	3k	2k	k	k

$3k + 2k + k + k = 7k = 1$ so $k = \frac{1}{7}$

C Cumulative distribution function (p 87)

C1 (a) 0.75 **(b)** 1 **(c)** 0.50 **(d)** 0.70

C2 (a) 0.75 **(b)** 0.20 **(c)** 0.50 **(d)** 0.40

C3 (a) 0.20 **(b)** 0.90 **(c)** 0.05 **(d)** 1 **(e)** 1

Exercise C (p 88)

1 (a) 0.7 **(b)** 0.9 **(c)** 0.7 **(d)** 0

2

x	1	2	3	4
F(x)	0.15	0.40	0.70	1

3

x	1	2	3	4	5
P(X = x)	0.1	0.1	0.2	0.3	0.3

4 (a) $\frac{1}{25} + \frac{2}{25} + \frac{3}{25} + \frac{4}{25} + \frac{5}{25} + \frac{4}{25} + \frac{3}{25} + \frac{2}{25} + \frac{1}{25}$
$= \frac{25}{25} = 1$

(b) $\frac{15}{25} = \frac{3}{5} = 0.6$

5 (a) 18 **(b)** $\frac{15}{18} = \frac{5}{6}$

6 (a) 0.05 **(b)** 0.8

7 (a) $\frac{1}{60}$ **(b)** $\frac{11}{12}$

D Mean, variance and standard deviation (p 90)

D1 1.15

D2 0.9; you will lose an average of 10p per game.

D3 (a)

y	0	1	10
P(Y = y)	0.75	0.2	0.05

(b) 0.7 **(c)** Better

D4 (a)

x	−10	5	20
$P(X = x)$	$\frac{5}{9}$	$\frac{5}{18}$	$\frac{1}{6}$

(b) $-\frac{5}{6}$; on average, Carl loses $\frac{5}{6}$p for every game they play.

D5 (a)

y	−10	20	50
$P(Y = y)$	$\frac{3}{4}$	$\frac{1}{8}$	$\frac{1}{8}$

(b) $\frac{5}{4} = 1.25$; on average, Carl wins 1.25p for every game they play.

D6 (a) The mean score for both games is 1.9.

(b) The distribution for game A is more spread out than that for game B.

D7 Because the total probability is 1

D8 Variance = 0.79, standard deviation = 0.89
Game A has the wider variation.
The graph for B is more concentrated around the centre (or less spread out).

Exercise D (p 93)

1 (a) 3.5   (b) 2.92 (to 3 s.f.)
(c) 1.71 (to 3 s.f.)

2 (a) $\frac{70}{36} = 1.94$ (to 3 s.f.)   (b) 2.05 (to 3 s.f.)
(c) 1.43 (to 3 s.f.)

3 (a)

x	1	2	3
$P(X = x)$	$\frac{1}{2}$	$\frac{3}{8}$	$\frac{1}{8}$

(b) $\frac{13}{8} = 1.625$ (c) 0.484 (to 3.s.f)

4 $E(X) = \frac{55}{15} = 3.67$, $Var(X) = 1.56$

5 (a) $k = \frac{1}{50}$ (b) $E(X) = 2$
(c) $Var(X) = 0.92$

6 (a) $E(X) = 3$, $Var(X) = 2$
(b) $E(Y) = 5.5$ (c) $\frac{n+1}{2}$

7 (a) $\beta = 0.1$, $\alpha = 0.2$ (b) 0.84

8 (a) $\alpha = 0.1$, $\beta = 0.3$ (b) 0.96

E Functions of a discrete random variable (p 94)

E1 (a) $E(X) = 2.5$, $Var(X) = 1.25$
(b) $E(Y) = 5$, $Var(Y) = 5$
(c) (i) $E(Y) = 2E(X)$ (ii) $Var(Y) = 4Var(X)$

E2 (a)

w	4	5	6	7
$P(W = w)$	$\frac{1}{4}$	$\frac{1}{4}$	$\frac{1}{4}$	$\frac{1}{4}$

(b) $E(W) = 5.5$, $Var(W) = 1.25$
(c) $E(W) = E(X) + 3$
(d) $Var(W) = Var(X)$

E3 (a)

v	5	7	9	11
$P(V = v)$	$\frac{1}{4}$	$\frac{1}{4}$	$\frac{1}{4}$	$\frac{1}{4}$

(b) $E(V) = 8$, $Var(V) = 5$
(c) (i) $E(V) = 2E(X) + 3$ (ii) $Var(V) = 4Var(X)$

Exercise E (p 96)

1 (a) 7.5   (b) 8   (c) 5   (d) 11.25

2 (a) 13.5   (b) 22.5   (c) 17.5   (d) 22.5
(e) −9   (f) 10   (g) −2   (h) 10

3 (a) $E(X) = 2.3$, $Var(X) = 0.81$
(b) (i) 8.9   (ii) 8.2   (iii) 3.24

4 (a) $\frac{1}{20}$ (b) $E(X) = 3.6$, $Var(X) = 0.34$
(c) (i) 8.2   (ii) 3.8   (iii) 1.36

5 (a) 2.25   (b) 6.25   (c) 1.1875   (d) 4.75

6 $a = 3, b = 6$ or $a = -3, b = 54$

Mixed questions (p 97)

1 (a) 3.1   (b) 1.29   (c) 0.9   (d) 11.3   (e) 5.16

2 (a) $\frac{1}{50}$ (b) 5.2   (c) 1.08   (d) 0.86   (e) 13.6

3 (a)

x	1	2	3	4	5	6
$P(X = x)$	0.09	0.09	0.09	0.09	0.09	0.55

(b) $E(X) = 4.65$, $Var(X) = 3.1275$

4 (a) 0.3   (b) 2.6   (c) 1.44

5 (a) $\alpha = 0.05$, $\beta = 0.45$ (b) 3.85
(c) 1.1275   (d) 2.3   (e) 4.51

6 (a) $\alpha = 0.15$, $\beta = 0.25$ **(b)** 1.8

   (c) 1.79   **(d)** 5.1   **(e)** 1.79

7 (a) $E(X) = 20b + 0.45$

   (b) $a = 0.8225$, $b = 0.0275$

   (c) £0.35

8 (a) (i) 1.8   **(ii)** 12.66   **(iii)** 1.75   **(iv)** 24.3875

   (b) Machine A, as the value of $E(X)$ is higher

   (c) Machine A: 20p; machine B: 25p

   (d) There is a bigger chance of getting £20 or nothing on machine B.

Test yourself (p 99)

1 (a) 0.2   **(b)** 0.4   **(c)** 0.3   **(d)** 0.2   **(e)** 8.96

2 (a)

x	1	2	3	4	5	6
$P(X = x)$	$\frac{1}{6}$	$\frac{1}{6}$	$\frac{1}{6}$	$\frac{1}{6}$	$\frac{1}{6}$	$\frac{1}{6}$

   (b) Uniform   **(c)** 16   **(d)** $\frac{140}{3}$

3 (a)

x	4	5	6
$P(X = x)$	$7k$	$16k$	$27k$

   $7k + 16k + 27k = 50k$ is equal to 1, so $k = \frac{1}{50}$.

   (b) $E(X) = 5\frac{2}{5} = 5.4$, $Var(X) = \frac{13}{25} = 0.52$

   (c) $Var(2X - 3) = 4 \times \frac{13}{25} = 2\frac{2}{25} = 2.08$

4 (a) $\frac{1}{2}$ **(b)** $\frac{17}{36}$ **(c)** $\frac{5}{6}$

5 (a)

x	1	2	3	4	5	6	7	8
$P(X = x)$	0.1	0.1	0.05	0.15	0.1	0.1	0.15	0.25

   (b) $E(X) = 5.2$
$$Var(X) = (1^2 \times 0.1) + (2^2 \times 0.1) + (3^2 \times 0.05)$$
$$+ (4^2 \times 0.15) + (5^2 \times 0.1) + (6^2 \times 0.1)$$
$$+ (7^2 \times 0.15) + (8^2 \times 0.25) - 5.2^2$$
$$= 32.8 - 27.04 = 5.76$$

   (c) $E(Y) = 13.4$, $Var(X) = 4 \times 5.76 = 23.04$

7 Normal distribution

Edexcel tables are used for these answers.
Other tables may give slightly different answers.

A Proportions (p 101)

A1 mean – 3 s.d. = 6.820
mean – 2 s.d. = 6.919
mean – 1 s.d. = 7.018
mean + 2 s.d. = 7.315
mean + 3 s.d. = 7.414

A2 (a) There are 34 values greater than 7.117 g and less than 7.216 g, which is 34% of all the coin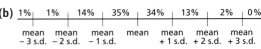

   (b)

1%	1%	14%	35%	34%	13%	2%	0%
mean – 3 s.d.	mean – 2 s.d.	mean – 1 s.d.	mean	mean + 1 s.d.	mean + 2 s.d.	mean + 3 s.d.	

A3

0%	3.3%	13.3%	33.3%	32.5%	16.7%	0.8%	0%
mean – 3 s.d.	mean – 2 s.d.	mean – 1 s.d.	mean	mean + 1 s.d.	mean + 2 s.d.	mean + 3 s.d.	

A4

0%	0%	25%	23.8%	28.8%	22.5%	0%	0%
mean – 3 s.d.	mean – 2 s.d.	mean – 1 s.d.	mean	mean + 1 s.d.	mean + 2 s.d.	mean + 3 s.d.	

A5 The first two are roughly symmetrical with a ver distinct peak between (mean – 1 s.d.) and (mean + 1 s.d.) In the third, the data is fairly evenly spread between the middle four classes.

A6 (a) Mean – 1 s.d. = 157 cm   **(b)** 181 cm

Exercise A (p 103)

1 (a) 16%   **(b)** 68%   **(c)** 2 people **(d)** 21

2 (a) 2%   **(b)** 34%   **(c)** 130

B The standard normal probability distribution

Exercise B (p 107)

1 (a) 0.7734   **(b)** $1 - 0.9678 = 0.0322$

   (c) 0.8944   **(d)** $0.9641 - 0.6915 = 0.2726$

2 (a) Sketch of normal curve
$0.9641 - 0.5 = 0.4641$

   (b) Sketch of normal curve
$0.9998 - 0.8944 = 0.1054$

   (c) Sketch of normal curve
$0.8023 - (1 - 0.9332) = 0.7355$

(d) Sketch of normal curve
$(1 − 0.8554) − (1 − 0.9925) = 0.1371$

3 (a) 0.0808 **(b)** 0.2420 **(c)** 0.7800

(d) 0.3023 **(e)** 0.5746 **(f)** 0.2798

4 Using the nearest value in the table:

(a) 1.64 or 1.65 **(b)** 1.28 **(c)** 2.32

(d) 0.67

5 (a) 0.84 **(b)** 1.04 **(c)** −0.25 **(d)** −0.13

6 (a) 0.44 **(b)** 0.81

C Finding probabilities and proportions

Exercise C (p 110)

1 $X \sim N(10, 2^2)$

(a) $z = 2.5$, $\Phi(2.5) = 0.9938$
$P(X > 15) = P(Z > 2.5) = 1 − 0.9938 = 0.0062$
So 0.6% of batteries fail after 15 hours.

(b) $P(8 \le X \le 12) = P(−1 \le Z \le 1)$
$\Phi(1.0) = 0.8413$
$P(8 \le X \le 12) = 0.8413 − (1 − 0.8413)$
$= 0.6826$
68% of batteries have a lifetime of between 8 and 12 hours.

2 $X \sim N(1.5, 0.01^2)$
$z = 2.0$, $\Phi(2.0) = 0.9772$
$P(X > 1.52) = P(Z > 2.0) = 1 − 0.9772 = 0.0228$
So 2.28% of bolts are rejected.

3 $X \sim N(100, 15^2)$
$z = 2.13$, $\Phi(2.13) = 0.9834$
$P(X > 132) = P(Z > 2.13) = 1 − 0.9834 = 0.0166$
So 1.66% of children have an IQ of 132 or more.

4 (a) 0.3085 **(b)** 0.0668 **(c)** 0.1359

5 $X \sim N(1.5, 0.01^2)$
$z = −2.5$, $\Phi(2.5) = 0.9938$
$P(X < 1.475) = P(Z < −2.5) = 1 − 0.9938$
$= 0.0062$

6 $X \sim N(500, 4^2)$
For $x = 500.5$, $z = 0.125$, $\Phi(0.125) = 0.5498$
For $x = 498.5$, $z = −0.375$, $\Phi(0.375) = 0.6462$
$P(498.5 < X < 500.5) = 0.5498 − (1 − 0.6462)$
$= 0.1960$

7 $X \sim N(154.2, 5.1^2)$
For $x = 155$, $z = 0.16$, $\Phi(0.16) = 0.5636$
For $x = 150$, $z = −0.82$, $\Phi(0.82) = 0.7939$
$P(150 < X < 155) = 0.5636 − (1 − 0.7939)$
$= 0.3575$

8 (a) 0.2743 **(b)** 0.3108

9 (a) Distinction: $1 − \Phi(2.33) = 0.0099$
Credit: $\Phi(2.33) = \Phi(0.67) = 0.2415$
Pass: $\Phi(0.67) − \Phi(−1.83) = 0.7150$
Fail: $\Phi(−1.83) = 0.0336$

(b) Distinction: $0.0099 \times 90 = 1$ person
Credit: $0.2415 \times 90 = 22$ people
Pass: $0.7150 \times 90 = 64$ people
Fail: $0.0336 \times 90 = 3$ people

D Working backwards (p 111)

D1 233.55, so quote 233 g

D2 For a 90% symmetrical interval there should be 5% left at each end. The interval is therefore given by $\mu \pm 1.6449\sigma$, or from $174 − 1.6449 \times 8$ to $174 + 1.6449 \times 8$, namely from 160.84 cm to 187.16 cm.

Exercise D (p 113)

1 Using the percentage points table, when $p = 0.15$, $z = 1.0364$
Mark $= 47 + 1.0364 \times 12 = 59.4$
so 60 must be achieved

2 Using the percentage points table, when $p = 0.1$, $z = 1.2816$
Mean $= 1 + 1.2816 \times 0.0025 = 1.003\,204$ kg

3 (a) $z = \dfrac{250 − 265}{10} = −1.5$
$\Phi(1.5) = 0.9332$
$P(X < 250) = P(Z < −1.5) = 1 − 0.9332$
$= 0.0668$

(b) 1 in 200 $= 0.005$
Using the percentage points table, when $p = 0.005$, $z = 2.5758$
So $\dfrac{250 − 265}{\sigma} = −2.5758$ which gives
$\sigma = 5.82$ ml

4 (a) $z = \dfrac{15 - 20}{3} = -1.67$

$\Phi(1.67) = 0.9525$

$P(X < 15) = P(Z < -1.67) = 1 - 0.9525$
$= 0.0475$

(b) Using the percentage points table, when
$p = 0.1$, $z = 1.2816$
Time $= 20 + 1.2816 \times 3 = 23.84$ minutes

(c) From the body of the table for $\Phi(z)$, when
$\Phi(z) = 0.9332$, $z = 1.5$
$\mu = 10 - 1.5 \times 4 = 4$ minutes

5 To have a 95% symmetrical interval there must
be 2.5% of values left at each end.
Using the percentage points table, when
$p = 0.025$, $z = 1.9600$
The interval is $80 \pm 1.96 \times 7$, namely from
66.28 cm to 93.72 cm.

6 Using the percentage points table, when $p = 0.1$,
$z = 1.2816 \approx 1.3$, so $\mu + 1.3\sigma = 70$
When $p = 0.15$, $z = 1.0364 \approx 1.0$, so $\mu - \sigma = 35$
Solving these gives $\sigma = 15.2$ and $\mu = 50.2$

7 $\mu - 0.75\sigma = 21.2$
$\mu + 1.25\sigma = 30$
$\mu = 24.5$, $\sigma = 4.4$

8 $1 - 0.055 = 0.945$ and from the table of $\Phi(z)$,
when $\Phi(z) = 0.945$, $z \approx 1.6$
So $\mu + 1.6\sigma = 165$
$1 - 0.115 = 0.885$ and from the table of $\Phi(z)$,
when $\Phi(z) = 0.885$, $z \approx 1.2$
So $\mu - 1.2\sigma = 140$
Solving these gives $\sigma = 8.93$ g and $\mu = 150.7$ g

9 (a) Using the percentage points table, when
$p = 0.2$, $z = 0.8416$
Diameter $= 224 + 0.8416 \times 4 = 227.4$ mm.

(b) Since this is 80% of the original distribution
the median m is such that $P(X < m) = 0.4$.
Using $p = 0.4$ in the percentage points table
gives $z = 0.2533$, but the required value is in
the left-hand tail, where $z = -0.2533$.
Median $= 224 - 0.2533 \times 4 = 223.0$ mm

Mixed questions (p 115)

1 0.2805

2 1 in $1000 = 0.001$
When $\Phi(z) = 0.999$, $z = 3.0902$
So quoted weight $= 265 - 3.09 \times 7 = 243$ g

3 (a) $P(X < 290) = \Phi\left(\dfrac{290 - 275}{15}\right) = \Phi(1.0)$
$= 0.8413$

$P(X < 260) = \Phi\left(\dfrac{260 - 275}{15}\right) = \Phi(-1.0)$
$= 1 - 0.8413 = 0.1587$

$P(260 < X < 290) = 0.8413 - 0.1587 = 0.682$

(b) $P(X > 300) = 1 - \Phi\left(\dfrac{300 - 275}{15}\right) = 1 - \Phi(1.6$
$= 1 - 0.9525 = 0.0475$

4 (a) $z = \dfrac{0.0155 - 0.0158}{0.002} = -0.15$

$P(Z < -0.15) = 1 - \Phi(0.15) = 1 - 0.5596$
$= 0.4404$

(b) 0.0138 mm

5 $\mu + 0.5\sigma = 8.7$, $\mu + 1.5\sigma = 11.1$, $\mu = 7.5$, $\sigma = 2.4$

6 $V \sim N(475, 20^2)$

(a) (i) $z = \dfrac{480 - 475}{20} = 0.25$
$\Phi(0.25) = 0.5987$
$P(V < 480) = 0.5987$

(ii) $P(460 < V < 490) = P(-0.75 < Z < 0.75)$
$\Phi(0.75) = 0.7734$
$P(460 < V < 480) = 0.7734 - (1 - 0.7734)$
$= 0.5468$

(b) $z = \dfrac{500 - 475}{20} = 1.25$
$\Phi(1.25) = 0.8944$
$P(V > 500) = 1 - 0.8944 = 0.1056$

(c) When $\Phi(z) = 1 - 0.001 = 0.999$, $z = 3.09$
$\mu = 500 - 3.09 \times 20 = 438.2$ ml

Test yourself (p 116)

1 0.6247

2 (a) 3.90 ml   **(b)** 6.18%   **(c)** 55.88 m

3 (a) 0.2912   **(b)** 4.640

4 (a) $15 = \mu + 1.6449\sigma$, $9 = \mu + 1.2816\sigma$
$\mu = 11.63$ hours, $\sigma = 2.05$ hours

(b) 78.8%

Index